Everyday Music

Wes Westmoreland and his son, Tanner Westmoreland, Lamkin, Texas, December 21, 2010.

JOHN AND ROBIN DICKSON SERIES IN TEXAS MUSIC

Sponsored by the
Center for Texas Music History

Texas State University–San Marcos

Gary Hartman, General Editor

A list of titles in this series is available at the back of the book

Fiddler Stacey Dodd and guitarist Tom Fonville, 78th Old Fiddlers Contest and Reunion, Athens, Texas, May 28, 2009

Everyday Music

ALAN GOVENAR

Online Education Guide by Paddy Bowman

TEXAS A&M UNIVERSITY PRESS   •   COLLEGE STATION

Texas Swing Festival and Old Fiddlers'
Reunion, Athens, Texas, May 27, 2009

Library of Congress Cataloging-in-Publication Data

Govenar, Alan B., 1952–
    Everyday music / Alan Govenar. — 1st ed.
        p. cm. — (John and Robin Dickson series in Texas music)
    Includes bibliographical references and index.
    Summary: During the 1980's and again from 2009–2011, folk-
lorist Alan Govenar traveled all over the state of Texas to interview
local performers of traditional music of all types and to make
recordings of this music. Many of these recordings were aired
on the "Traditional music of Texas" radio program.
    ISBN 978-1-60344-528-3 (cloth : alk. paper) —
    ISBN 1-60344-528-5 (cloth : alk. paper) —
    ISBN 978-1-60344-756-0 (e-book) —
    ISBN 1-60344-756-3 (e-book)
    1. Folk music—Texas—History and criticism.   2. Folk musi-
cians—Texas—Biography.   3. Folk musicians—Texas—Interviews.
4. Texas—Social life and customs—20th century.   5. Texas—Social
life and customs—21st century.   6. Texas—Biography.
I. Traditional music in Texas.   II. Title.
III. Series: John and Robin Dickson series in Texas music.
    ML3551.7.T35G38   2012
    781.62009764—dc23
    2011048841

Map on page 8 by Daniel S. Dunnam   *Unless otherwise indicated, all photographs are by Alan Govenar.*

Alan Govenar recording the
Original Oompah Band, Tivydale,
Texas, September 1, 1986, Courtesy
Fredericksburg Standard-Radio Post

A special online resource for this book, which includes an education
guide and other instructional aids, as well as photographs, audio recordings,
and videos, is available at www.everydaymusiconline.org.

Wes Westmoreland practicing a fiddle
tune before competing in the 78th Old
Fiddlers Contest and Reunion, Athens,
Texas, May 28, 2009

Contents

J. W. Stoker, Weatherford, Texas, 1984

Driving to Athens, Texas, May 28, 2009

Introduction

Texas FM 813, April 16, 2011

ON US HIGHWAY 175 south of Dallas, thunderheads push across hazy sky, darkening the landscape with heavy shadows. The air is hot and sticky. Huge drops of rain spatter in a staccato beat on the hood of my car, fogging the interior glass so quickly that I can hardly see. I slow down to pull off the road and skid onto the gravel shoulder. After about fifteen minutes, the storm subsides. Sun streaks through the clouds in front of me as the steady rhythm of the wipers on my dripping windshield keeps time with the music now running through my head.

Between 1983 and 1988 I traveled more than thirty-five thousand miles around Texas, not all at once, but on different trips. I'd usually venture out for three or four days, but sometimes I'd leave for a week or two. I camped, stayed in motels, and visited friends. Mostly, I was alone, and the time by myself was exactly what I needed. I was hungry for the open road.

I tried to blend in, but no matter how much I tried, my Boston accent usually slipped out and made it very clear that I was from some place faraway. One time, an old cowboy with leathery skin in a truck stop café even asked me in a heavy drawl if I was speaking Spanish. Embarrassed, I shook my head no and turned away. I wasn't looking for trouble.

I was doing fieldwork for a radio series called *Traditional Music in Texas* for the National Public Radio station in Dallas. I had a sense of what I might find based on my research and recordings that others had made, but often I didn't know exactly what to expect. I'd stop in a town or in the middle of an inner-city neighborhood and start talking to people at gas stations, or restaurants, or little grocery stores. In nightclubs, VFW Halls, and lodges that hosted dances, I'd ask questions about local music. I was looking for performers whose music was rooted in their cultural backgrounds. Whether or not they were profes-

Trio Los Olmos recording songs in the living room of their home for the *Traditional Music in Texas* radio series, Fort Worth, Texas, February 1984

sionals didn't matter. I was collecting folklore, the time-honored songs, stories, poems, and other oral traditions that had been passed on from one generation to another by word of mouth, most often through families and people in the communities where the musicians lived and worked.

Everyday Music begins where I left off years ago. I selected the people for this book because they made such a strong impression when I first met them. Reconnecting seemed like a good idea, although I soon discovered many had died. Some of the musical traditions they embraced had lost their appeal. Others have taken new directions.

As I near Athens, the landscape thickens with trees—pine, poplar, red oak, and cherry laurel—scattered across the sandy soil and rolling pastures of native grass and Texas buttercups. The town's Old Fiddlers Contest and Reunion, started in 1932, is held annually on the lawn of the Henderson County Courthouse on the last Friday in May. People begin gathering in the morning. They bring picnic baskets, spread blankets, and unfold chairs, staking out their places in the shade of the towering hardwood trees on the square. By noon, more than three hundred people of all ages are in the audience. Fiddle cases lie open near a makeshift covered stage on a flat-bed trailer, sandwiched between concession stands selling everything from snow cones, funnel cakes, and homemade ice cream to barbecue beef, ribs, turkey legs, and East Texas sausage links.

Contestants range in age from six to eighty-five, and the competition is broken into five divisions, each with its own prizes, varying from $200 to $500. The judges assess the bowing technique, tempo, tune selection, and contestant's understanding of the old-time fiddling sound.

On the street about fifty yards from the stage, I see Howard Dee "Wes" Westmoreland III. He's practicing with two of his friends, readying himself for the competition. I haven't talked to Wes since he was a teenager in the mid-1980s. "I got here in time to sign up in the 65 and Under Division," he says. "I just got in, and I'm thankful I did."

Wes first competed in the Texas Fiddlers Contest and Reunion when he was ten years old, and over the years, he has returned often. In 2009, he won his division and was named grand champion for his performance of the breakdown "Tom and Jerry," a tune he repeats this year to loud applause. The judges

78th Old Fiddlers Contest and Reunion, Athens, Texas, May 28, 2009

Texas FM 813, April 16, 2011

score his performance high; his timing is meticulous, his bow work fluid and compelling. Once again, he wins his division and is crowned grand champion. Westmoreland is all smiles. "If you listened to a recording of how I played the same song last year, it would be different. The music morphs from performance to performance, generation to generation. Everyone brings their own touch."

For a tradition to continue it must be fulfilling for musicians and listeners alike. The life of a tradition depends on interaction and communication within the families and communities in which the music is performed. Traditional music expresses shared beliefs and group experience, which may be defined by culture, religion, language, gender, region, or occupation. In some instances, musical traditions may be dormant among one generation and be revived in a new form by the next. In this book I explore the development of different styles of music and the ways in which they are learned and remembered. By revisiting the subjects of my earlier work, I have a gained a greater sense of how the meaning of a tradition can change over time.

At the Tigua Indian Reservation on the outskirts of El Paso, for example, twenty-five years after I interviewed Miguel Pedraza Sr. in his home, I met with tribal historian Javier Loera. I brought the recordings I had made hoping to learn more about Pedraza's chants. Loera listened and then looked up. "These chants I had only heard about, but had never heard. Some are religious in nature and should not have been made public. But Mr. Pedraza trusted you, and I'm glad he did. These recordings preserve our culture. Without the knowledge of our culture, there are no Tigua." I didn't know what to say. I had not fully realized the extent to which a single interview could have such importance in helping one generation to connect with the next.

Javier Loera, Tribal Historian, Ysleta del Sur Pueblo, El Paso, Texas, April 15, 2011

Texas FM 813, April 16, 2011

Narciso and Edwina Martínez, San Benito, Texas, April, 1985

Each chapter of this book starts in the mid-1980s. The opening paragraphs are told in the present tense as journal accounts based on the field notes I made during my road trips around Texas. In the second part of each chapter, the tone is more biographical and combines interviews I conducted in the 1980s with those done between 2009 and 2011. The photographs throughout the text also reflect the juxtaposition of then and now, drawing from archival or historical sources, family snapshots, and my own work.

While the featured musicians reflect the vast cultural landscape of Texas, they are by no means all-inclusive. In Texas, traditional music has developed a distinctive character that results from the cross-pollination of regional musical styles—itself a result of the migratory patterns into the state—from the earliest Native American tribes to French and Spanish settlers, Mexicans, Anglo/Europeans, African Americans, and Asians. In addition, changes in the recording industry, radio, and television have had a profound impact on musicians and their listeners. Living traditions are constantly evolving; they are both old and new. Individual performers may excel in different musical styles. Wes Westmoreland began his career playing the fiddle tunes he learned from his grandfather. As he got older, he began performing in Western swing bands, but he has now returned to his musical roots in fiddle contests around the state.

Other musicians, whom I recorded for the *Traditional Music in Texas* radio series, also demonstrate how musical traditions change. In Groves, Texas, near the Louisiana border, Allen Thibodeaux and the French Ramblers fused Cajun music with country and western dance sounds. In San Benito, Narciso Martínez, considered the father of what today is known as Mexican American *norteño* music, transcribed the songs he heard farm workers whistling to the accordion, an instrument brought to the state by German immigrants in the 1840s.

The accordion, like the fiddle, is one of the dominant instruments in the traditional music of Texas. Musicians of Mexican American, Czech, German, Irish, Jewish, Cajun, and Creole descent all play the accordion. Each culture uses different kinds of accordions. For example, Narciso Martínez used a one-row button accordion when he began playing dances in the late 1920s, and he later purchased a two-row button accordion in the 1930s and a three-row button accordion in the 1940s. In the next generation, Valerio Longoria, while influenced by Martínez, expanded the instrumentation of his *conjunto* (band) to

Driving through Austin, Texas, May 6, 2011

feature guitar, stand-up bass, and a drum-set in addition to the accordion. Since the 1970s and 1980s, electric instruments, saxophones, and modern percussion have been added to *norteño* music. Current songs draw upon traditional forms, but the lyrics composed by younger musicians reflect the attitudes and beliefs of their peers. To remain vital, *norteño,* like other styles of traditional music, continues to reinvent itself.

The interactive website that accompanies this book, www.everydaymusic online.org, contains an education guide and provides additional photographs, audio recordings, and videos to highlight the traditions discussed in each chapter and explores their connection to other styles of music in the thirty-nine-part radio series I recorded and produced in the 1980s. Overall, the website elaborates the kaleidoscope of cultures and musical styles found in the state, from contest fiddling, blues, polka, zydeco, and *norteño* to Cajun music, Yiddish songs, Kiowa flute, and Sacred Harp singing. *Everyday Music* is a musical journey through Texas. The stories that people tell and the music they perform continue to have great resonance for their communities, families, descendants, and us all.

South of Floresville, Texas, May 7, 2011

Everyday Music

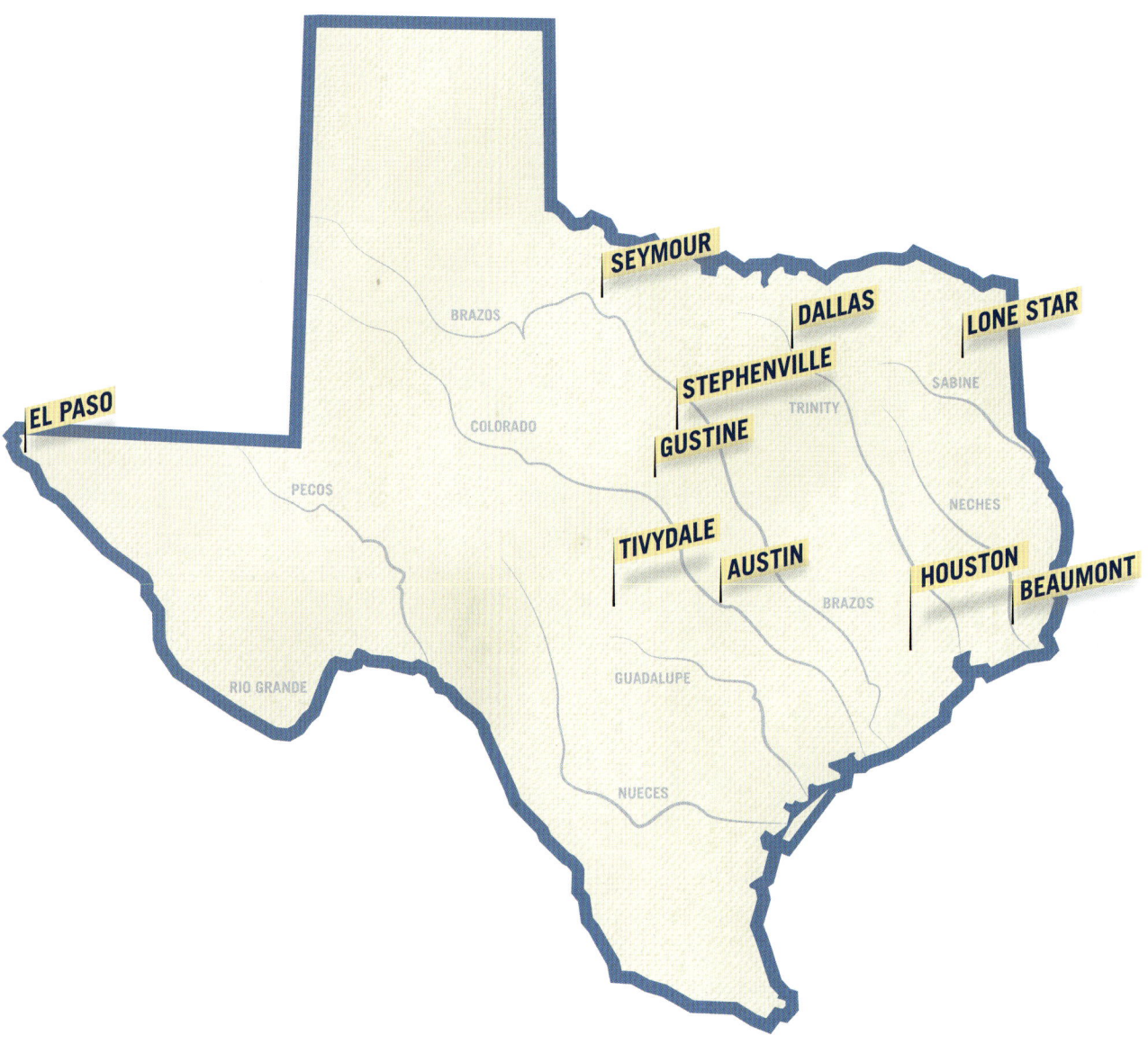

Julius Vita

Czech Accordion, Seymour

Inside Wicker Feed Store on the south side of the Baylor County Courthouse Square in Seymour during the second week of July, conversation centers on family, livestock, and the Old Settlers Reunion and Rodeo, the oldest event of its kind in Texas. Started by a retired cowboy named Jeff Scott in July 1896, the first three-day reunion included a rodeo, a barbecue, baseball games, and a Grand Ball. Hundreds of people came, and it was so successful that the town leaders decided to organize another. The Cowboy Reunion of 1897 was bigger than the first and was attended by Comanche Chief Quanah Parker and some three

Driving to Seymour, Texas, July 12, 1984

Wicker Feed Store, Seymour, Texas,
July 13, 1984

hundred members of his tribe. One night they even staged an Indian War Dance
around a bonfire, dressed in full battle regalia. Over the years, the Old Settlers
Reunion and Rodeo, as it is now called, has continued to grow and now even at-
tracts cowboys on the Professional Rodeo Cowboy Association (PRCA) circuit.

Wicker's has the feel of a general store, where locals shop, swap stories, and
joke around. When I ask about traditional music, a short, white-haired man who
looks to be in his sixties ambles up to the counter and introduces himself as Julius Vita. "I do a little of that myself," he says with a half-smile. "I play accordion
and sing the old Czech songs. Interested?"

"Definitely," I reply, surprised to find a Czech accordion player in a Texas feed
store.

Vita is pleased and has a little kick in his step as he exits the store to get his
accordion from the back seat of his red Ford Bronco parked next to my Honda
Civic. He owns an auto parts store on Main Street, and Wicker's is one of his
favorite stops after lunch or when he's out doing errands around town. Back
inside, everyone waits in anticipation. Charles Wicker moves a chair into place
and Vita sits down. The first song is a waltz, and when he's done, I ask if I can

interview him and record some of his playing. He nods and says, "If you got nerves enough to stick with me."

I rush out to my car and bring in a tape recorder and thread a reel-to-reel tape as fast as I can. Vita scratches his head, quietly amused by the equipment set up in front of him, then pulls the bellows of his accordion and picks up where he left off as he segues into a fast polka.

Julius Vita performing in Wicker Feed Store, Seymour, Texas, July 13, 1984

JULIUS VITA was born January 25, 1918, in Bomarton, Texas, about ten miles due west of Seymour. His parents had emigrated from Czechoslovakia through Galveston to the town of East in Central Texas before buying a farm in 1928 in Bomarton, a small farming community of mostly Czech immigrants in Baylor County. Tim Orsak, a local historian who works as an operations manager at the Seymour Independent School District, says that the first Czechs came to Bomarton around 1908, searching for "cheap land," and that the community grew to about 150 Czech families by 1915 but then rapidly declined because of a terrible drought. "By 1917," Orsak recalls, "over eighty families had left, though there was still a strong Czech presence in language and music. In the 1920s the Bomarton Brass Band was well-known in the area, and later, Anton Kohut organized a fourteen-piece Czech band."

As a boy, Julius Vita attended a one-room schoolhouse in Mary's Creek, a small town near his home, but he quit in the seventh grade because his father was gravely ill and his help was needed on the farm. He started playing music around the age of six, learning from his father and brothers, and at sixteen, his mother bought him an accordion.

"My mother promised me that if I didn't smoke until I was eighteen years old," he recalled, "she'd buy me an accordion. I had been smoking cedar bark,

Julius Vita performing in Wicker Feed Store, Seymour, Texas, July 13, 1984

Entrance to Seymour Rodeo Grounds,
Seymour, Texas, July 14, 1984

anything I could get a hold of, out behind the barn, but I really didn't like it. And when she told me, I'd already seen that I didn't like to smoke, so I just gave it up completely. I didn't even try to smoke. So, I told her I'm sixteen now and I'm not figuring on starting smoking. So, she bought me an accordion."

Growing up, Vita never joined a band per se but instead played at local barn dances, where he might have fiddle and guitar accompaniment. "They'd clean out the barn and dance on the dirt floor," Julius' son Jim Vita says. "All the musicians were like him. They worked day jobs. Whoever was available showed up to play. In fact, my folks met at a barn dance and married in 1944. Mom was from Rhineland, about twenty miles west of Bomarton. Her maiden name was Margaret Birkenfield and she was of German descent."

The barn dances mixed polkas and waltzes with Czech folksongs. "I know quite a few of them," Julius said, "but I don't remember the names." One of his most requested songs was the waltz "Louka Zelena" ("Green Meadow") and "Julida Polka," which was also popular in German immigrant communities around Texas. Other Czech songs included the melancholy "A Ja Sam" ("I Alone") and tunes about love and the beauty of nature, such as "Na Bilej Hore" ("On White Mountain") and "Pod Dubem, Za Dubem" ("Over the Oak, Under the Oak").

Over the years, Vita performed mainly at informal gatherings of his family

88th Old Settlers Reunion and Rodeo,
Seymour, Texas, July 14, 1984

and friends in the Czech communities in Bomarton and Seymour. Tim Orsak recalls hearing Vita for the first time in the church hall at the Sacred Heart Catholic Church when he was about 10 years old: "He was sitting by himself near where the band had been playing. The band was on break. There were no Czech bands in Seymour at the time, but we had a lot that came through from the Dallas–Fort Worth area—the Panther City Polka Boys, the Alpine Village Band, the Czech Harvesters, Jodie Mikula, and even the Vrazels played here. Sometimes Mr. Vita sat in, but mostly he liked to play by himself. He liked the old tunes he had heard growing up. He never sang, and I couldn't tell if he was playing the whole song, but everybody enjoyed it. Everyone around here liked him. He was a great supporter of all the kids, whether at athletic events or stock shows."

Vita was a lifetime member of the Veterans of Foreign Wars (VFW), a Third Degree Knight of Columbus, and an active member of the Sacred Heart Catholic Church. "About 70 percent of the church was Czech," Jim Vita says, "and Dad was a true volunteer. He'd play for people in the Westview Nursing Home and was instrumental in starting Little League Baseball in Seymour. Mom kept all the score cards and they did whatever they could to keep Little League going for about ten years."

Jim learned about Czech music from his father and started playing himself when he was about nine years old. "I would run home from church on Sunday

South of Seymour, Texas, July 15, 1984

mornings, and I'd mess around on the piano and then break out his old accordion before they got home. They'd want to sit around after church and talk to their friends. So, it gave me a chance to just pick things up about music here and there."

As he got older, Jim played in a band called The Tiger Tails, named after the fuzzy toy tiger tails given away by Esso (now Exxon Mobil) gas stations as a promotion. "We'd hang those tiger tails off the neck of our guitars. We had three guitars and a drummer, and we played local dances, every other week at the VFW Hall, everywhere around here. We didn't do any Czech songs. We were into country music—Patsy Cline, Johnny Cash, and a lot of Johnny Bush, whose big hit at that time was 'One Fool on a Stool.'"

One time, Julius Vita got his son Jim to play with him for an American Cancer Society benefit at the Seymour Golf Club and Country Club. They called themselves Hans and Franz and dressed in lederhosen and busked from table to table for five dollars a song. "We played a lot of songs," Jim says. "We raised about a thousand dollars."

Each year the Vita family reunion was timed to coordinate with the Old Settlers Reunion and Rodeo in Seymour. There were nine children in Julius Vita's family, seven girls and two boys, and five of the Vita girls married five Hrnicrik

Leaving West Texas, December 21, 2010

Driving toward Stephenville, Texas,
December 21, 2010

boys, all of whom were from Baylor County. "We'd get over two hundred people, brothers, sisters, children, grandchildren, and great grandchildren."

Jim Vita still has two of his father's three-button Hohner accordions: his first, bought by his mother, and his last, given to him as a gift by his wife and children on his fiftieth birthday. Jim remembers some of the old Czech tunes but wishes he knew more. "My family spoke Czech when they didn't want us to know what they were talking about," he says. "I hated that they didn't pass it down." Julius Vita died January 28, 1989.

Even though there are no longer Czech bands in Seymour, Czech music is still popular in Baylor County and memories of Julius Vita remain a source of pride in his community. A local radio station, based in Seymour, broadcasts polka music every Sunday from noon to 3 p.m. Station owner and manager Mark Aulabaugh says, "We do local programming from noon to 1 p.m. and then we air *It's Polka Time,* a syndicated show hosted by Craig Ebel that is produced in the Twin Cities of Minneapolis and St. Paul. KSEY FM reaches about five counties, though our primary listeners are in about a fifty-mile radius from Seymour—Munday, Knox City, and Benjamin. In addition to Czech music, we are eclectic—meaning classic Western swing, honky-tonk, and local country bands, though we are principally farm radio with in-depth weather reports, agriculture and ranching news, and agricultural commentary geared to our listeners who are farmers and ranchers."

John Burrus

Cowboy Songs and Country Hymns, Stephenville

In the riding arena behind his Depression-era stone house on the outskirts of Stephenville, John Burrus tugs on the reins of the chestnut quarter horse he is training. He turns to the right, then lopes in a circle and moves to the left. "Some horses don't know how to turn without tripping over the front foot," he says as he slows to a stop.

I tell Burrus that I'd heard about him from Fred Dalby, a rancher in Aspermont, and he rubs the back of his neck with the index finger of his right hand, not sure exactly how to respond.

Stephenville, Texas, December 20, 2010

John Burrus' house, Stephenville, Texas, December 20, 2010

"Fred told me that you sing some of the old cowboy songs," I explain.

In his blue denim shirt and jeans, scuffed work boots, and beaten-up black felt hat cocked forward on his brow, Burrus is stocky and muscular, stoic but soft-spoken, a man of measured words.

"I roped with Fred all over West Texas," he nods. "Yeah, I've been all over the United States rodeoing. I've done all right. All I can do now is breakaway and ribbon roping. I can't get off the horse and tie the calf any more. My knees and ankles are all tore up. That ain't so hard. It's the breakin' and trainin' them

John Burrus, Stephenville, Texas, 1986

horses. What I do for a living. Everybody brings me those outlaw horses, and they rear and fall, buck me off, fall on me. It takes about thirty days where you can take a horse and ride it down the road and get him handling pretty good, but it takes a good while for a roping horse. All depends on the horse. Some horses train out fast, and some of them it takes a year or so. The trick is staying on their back with saddle blankets."

I follow him out of the arena across his backyard, shaded with mesquite and hackberry trees, to the kitchen door of his home. Inside, he leads me to the living room, where he offers me a seat across from the fireplace. Then he reaches for his guitar, perched in a stand behind the dining room table, grabs his harmonica rack and positions it around his neck, and hums before he starts to sing in a husky voice.

(below, left) John Burrus, Calcutta, India, December, 1945, Courtesy Gwen Burrus

(below) John Burrus (left) and his cousin Thomas Burrus, ca. 1946, Courtesy Gwen Burrus

John Burrus, December, 1949, Courtesy
Gwen Burrus

JOHN BURRUS was born December 29, 1923, in Eldorado, about forty-five miles south of San Angelo on US Highway 277. His grandparents, he said, "came to Texas from Missouri in a covered wagon. My father was a rancher, and I was raised breaking and training horses."

As a boy growing up, Burrus was interested in music. "My dad gave me a colt when I was about five or six years old, and when I was twelve, I traded that colt for a mandolin. My music teacher in Eldorado ordered me one. I took lessons for about a year. Then I traded my brother the trombone I played in high school for his guitar."

After graduating from high school, Burrus volunteered for the US Army and served during World War II in New Guinea and India until his discharge. When he returned to Texas, he worked on the ranch his father leased in Vance, and he played the guitar in his spare time. One day, when he was in town, he met Gwen Bain from nearby Barksdale. "John came to my grandfather's store to buy some ice," Gwen recalls, "and I happened to be working on that day." They married a

John and Gwen Burrus on their wedding
day, Uvalde, Texas, October 27, 1947,
Courtesy Gwen Burrus

year and a half later in October 1947. The couple moved to a ranch near Gold-waithe, Texas, and later to Comanche, where John broke and trained horses.

In the mid-1950s, John joined the Rodeo Cowboys Association (RCA) and competed professionally in calf-roping events not only in Texas but also in Utah, Wyoming, Idaho, Montana, North Dakota, and as far away as Calgary and Alberta, Canada. While on the road, John took his guitar and fiddle, and when

John Burrus roping a calf, Breckenridge, Texas, ca. early 1950s, Photograph by Richard Hodges, Courtesy Gwen Burrus

John Burrus, ca. 1950s, Courtesy Gwen
Burrus

John Burrus' wife Gwen Burrus, Stephenville, Texas, December 20, 2010

John Burrus roping a calf, Stephenville, Texas, ca. 1980s, Courtesy Gwen Burrus

John Burrus' son, Jamie Burrus, Stephenville, Texas, December 20, 2010

Jamie Burrus, Stephenville, Texas,
December 20, 2010

the other cowboys went into town, he stayed back at camp to read his Bible and practice his music. He knew a few basic chords, G, D, C, and A, and then tried singing along as he played. He remembered the traditional songs he had heard as a child. Later, he added new arrangements to his repertoire, based on songs he heard other cowboys sing and sheet music he had seen in songbooks and Christian hymnals. In time, he bought himself a harmonica. "I just picked it up and went to blowing it," he said. "It was a cowboy instrument, you bet. It's easy to pack. Ain't much room in the pocket of them jeans."

Sometimes at rodeos, Burrus would take his guitar and harmonica and sit in the stands while the cowboys were out riding around warming up their horses. "He'd even bring his Bible with him," Gwen recalled. "John was a devout Christian. He'd be there sometimes by himself before anybody else got there. The wives of the other cowboys appreciated that because they were sitting there waiting for their husbands to rope. And some of the guys riding around in the arena made fun of him. But the wives would ask him to pray for somebody they were concerned about. It got to where a lot of them would ask him to pray. He would just stand up, take his hat off, or maybe when he was just sitting there holding his guitar, he'd take his hat off and pray. He would say something like, 'Lord

Jesus, we thank you for all that you've done for us, and for saving us from our sins. We ask you to bless this person and heal the sickness in your own way.'"

In addition to rodeos, Burrus liked to perform in nursing homes for senior citizens and at camp meetings that were usually held in the summer. "John Gaither, a friend of his," Gwen says, "worked for the Four Sixes Ranch, near Guthrie. The meeting would be on someone's ranch and would last two or three nights. We took our motor home. They would put up a tent and would have someone bring the sermon. John would play his guitar and sing. A mix of cowboy songs and church songs. The service would last as long as they wanted it to, usually not more than an hour and a half, something like that. Some cowboys would stand up and give testimonials. I've seen tears in some of their eyes, but no one really broke down and cried. They would talk about what God had done for them, helped them through bad times. Sometimes it might be a broken marriage that got mended, or a child that had gone wayward that gotten straightened out, or some friend, just things that would affect their lives. It was never denominational, but it was Christian."

Texas CR 385, Stephenville, Texas, December 20, 2011

The songs John Burrus performed evoke the spirit of the working cowboy. The perils of herding cattle combine with the yearning for stability and faith in the uncertainties of life on the open range. Most of the songs have a moral— out of the hardship comes a higher purpose and, sometimes, salvation, "free from the burden of sin." "To me," Gwen says, "John was unusual. He had very high morals and that's what he wanted to sing about. But he also liked singing some of the old cowboy songs."

In "Windy Bill," a cowboy meets his match in a big black steer and learns a hard lesson. In "Trail to Mexico," after a cowboy leaves his "darling girl" and loses her to a "richer life," he laments, "Old buddy, old buddy, please stay at home. Don't be forever on the roam . . . God pity a girl that won't prove true. I'll travel west where the bullets fly, and I'll stay on the trail till the day I die."

In "Kentucky Waltz," a cowboy longs for the romance he had with the girl of his dreams: "Now I was a lad that was lucky, but it all ended too soon." "Power in the Blood" extols the strength faith imbues once a true commitment to the Lord is made: "Would you do service for Jesus, your king? There's power in the blood, power in the blood." "He Was Just a Lonely Cowboy" tells the story of a cowboy named Jack who falls in love with a "maiden," but prior to their wedding day, "a quarrel came between them" and Jack left. When he returns, he finds that she has already died: "They said as she was dying / She breathed her sweetheart's name / And told them with her last breath / To tell him when he came."

In 1973 Burrus bought an indoor arena and ninety-six acres of grazing land west of Stephenville, where his three sons and daughter helped him train horses and run the State 4-H Roping School. In 1986 he was forced to stop working with horses because of a leg injury, and his son William assumed the horse-breaking responsibilities.

While Burrus no longer worked on the ranch, he kept one horse, named "Shorty," which he sometimes took out to keep him "reining properly." During the last years of his life, he continued to play guitar, mandolin, fiddle, and harmonica at home, singing or humming to pass the time and to entertain his wife and family. John Burrus died December 26, 2009, but his legacy lives on. His sons, William and Jamie, and his two grandsons, William and Brant, whom he taught to play guitar, still sing many of the cowboy songs and country hymns they learned from him. Jamie Burrus, in addition to performing the traditional music he learned as a boy, is the pastor of a cowboy church in Bunger, Texas, and his brother, William performs in a band at a cowboy church in Stephenville.

Osceola Mays

Spirituals and Poems, Dallas

At the Good Street and Good Haven Community Center in South Dallas, Verna Raven leads a group of children in the hand-clapping game "Miss Mary Mack." When they finish, everyone is giggling; some are repeating the first verse:

> *Miss Mary Mack, Mack, Mack*
> *All dressed in black, black, black*
> *With silver buttons, buttons, buttons*
> *All down her back, back, back*

Looking toward downtown from South Dallas near Osceola Mays' house, April 16, 2011

Osceola Mays's house, 1309
Pennsylvania Avenue, Dallas, Texas,
April 16, 2011

Mrs. Raven steps to the side. I tell her about the 1983 Dallas Folk Festival and invite her and the children to perform. She smiles, "Sounds . . . fine, but I need to get all the parents to sign off for the children to participate." Then she pauses and says, "You must meet Mrs. Mays, a member of my church. She's exactly who you're looking for."

When I call Mrs. Mays, she answers the telephone with a timid voice and asks me to come to her house, which is about a ten-minute drive from the Community Center. When I get there, she is waiting for me, sitting on her porch

Osceola Mays reciting a poem at her dining room table, Dallas, Texas, September 13, 1984

Cotton pickers, Dallas County, Texas, ca. 1920s, Courtesy Texas/Dallas History and Archives Division, Dallas Public Library

swing with her husband, a lanky man with a ball cap and stubbly beard. She beckons me to follow her inside, but I am a little apprehensive. There is barbed wire strung across the front windows of their small wood-frame house.

Osceola Mays sits at her cluttered dining room table without moving. She closes her eyes and starts to say something, but then she covers her mouth with the palm of her hand as if to hold back her voice. There is a short pause before she begins to sing. The words come forth with a steady rhythm and her body sways forward and back. The notes are long and deep, calling forth the memories of spirituals she heard as a child—"Run, Sinner, Run," "Steal Away," and others come and go as the morning becomes afternoon. It is not "correct" singing, she says, offering me a glass of cold water from a plastic jug placed neatly on the table in front of her. Interspersed with her spirituals, she talks about her mother and grandmother and recites a few of the poems that she learned from them. She enunciates each word carefully as her voice rises and falls in a cadence that evokes a bygone era. The light from the window casts her face in darkness. The house feels different as the afternoon sun fills the front room, making the photographs and knickknacks around us seem more prominent. A pump organ covered with stacks of paper and 45-rpm records sits across from a brown and orange couch. On the walls are prints of a portrait of Jesus and a reproduction of Leonardo da Vinci's *Last Supper* near a Martin Luther King Jr. plate.

Clarence and Osceola Mays on their porch swing, Dallas, Texas, September 13, 1984

O SCEOLA MAYS was born December 13, 1909, in Waskom, a rural area of Northeast Texas near Marshall. Her earliest memories were of steamboats going down the river to pick up wood and cotton and of her brother getting lost in the woods and being found by people carrying torches of burning pine. Her strongest memory, though, was of getting her name when she was three or four years old. Until then she had simply been called "Sister" or "Garnell" after a white girl in town. "There was an Indian man traveling through Waskom," she said. "He stretched his tent right close to our house. Mama and Daddy would drink coffee with him. Sometimes he'd give me some cookies and candy . . . and I told Mama I wanted to be named for him. Mama said, 'No.' 'Well,' he said, 'that's all right. She can wear my name.' And I named myself Osceola. That was his name, and my name was after him."

When Osceola was six, her mother began teaching her spirituals and poems that had been passed on orally in her family from one generation to the next. "My mother would sit me down on the floor in the kitchen while she cooked," Osceola remembered, "and I'd repeat them after her."

When Osceola was ten, her mother died in childbirth, and from that time on, her father, Albert Douglas, and her grandmother, Laura Walker, raised her. Laura Walker was ten years old when the Emancipation Proclamation was signed to end slavery. She lived into her nineties, had seventeen children, and died on the day of a family reunion planned by her for more than one hundred grandchildren and great-grandchildren. Osceola loved to spend time with her grandmother, who not only taught her the domestic skills to make a living as cook, maid, or nanny but also instructed her in a style of singing and recitation that she kept over the course of her life.

Osceola's favorite spirituals were the most traditional, such as "Swing Low, Sweet Chariot," "Steal Away," and "Wade in the Water," all of which, her grandmother explained, may have had double meanings. "They were a way for the slaves to communicate with each other in code," she recalled, "without their masters knowing what they were really saying, but they also sang those spirituals because they expressed what they truly believed." For example, the coded meaning of the lyrics "Swing low, sweet chariot, comin' for to carry me home" was "Get ready. The chariot drivers (conductors on the Underground Railroad) are arriving soon." Similarly, "Steal away, steal away home, I ain't got long to stay here" was a signal to prepare to escape.

Like her grandmother, Osceola enjoyed singing spirituals a cappella (without instrumental accompaniment). The melodies moved slowly from note to note in her singing. Frequently, there was a rise in her voice at the beginning of a new verse or when she used an extended syllable or sang "Oh. . . ." in a long breath. She often had a sorrowful tone, repeating lines and phrases to accentuate the feelings of sadness, loss, and separation. The lament of earthly hardships was often offset by her musings about the peace of dying and the hope for eternal life.

A cappella spirituals were integral to Osceola's childhood, but as she got

(opposite) Osceola Mays' mother, Azalean Douglas, ca. 1917, Waskom, Texas, Courtesy Osceola Mays

Osceola Mays, Dallas, Texas, 1961,
Courtesy Osceola Mays

Osceola Mays (second from right) at
the wedding reception of Thelma Isaac
Thomas, Dallas, Texas, ca. late 1940s,
Courtesy Osceola Mays

Hand-tinted photo postcard of the
Good Street Baptist Church, where
Osceola was a member for more than
forty years, ca. 1950s, Courtesy Texas
African American Photography Archive

Osceola Mays performing at the Maison des Cultures du Monde, Paris, France, December 1989

Osceola Mays working as a nanny, Dallas, Texas, ca. 1950s, Courtesy Osceola Mays

older she became more interested in choir singing. Her creative impulse to write and recite poems, which was nurtured by her grandmother, was stifled by the demands of work and marriage. Osceola finished school in grade 11 in Waskom. In segregated African American schools, there wasn't a grade 12, and she was expected to get full-time work. She toiled long hours as a domestic maid in the homes of "white folks," cleaning, doing laundry, and babysitting. By the time she was seventeen, she said, "I started liking boys and boys would come see me. I lost interest in poems. I'd go to ball games and picnics, and I'd go to the store to buy ice cream. All of these things took my mind off poems and spirituals, but I never forgot what I already knew. I didn't write them down. I didn't have any need to write. I didn't get but one pencil and I used that up in school."

In 1935 Osceola met Clarence Mays, a hard-working cotton sharecropper who had been married once before and had a daughter named Lauretha. Osceola and Clarence married January 24, 1936. They wanted to go to the minister's

Osceola Mays performing at Spence Middle School, Dallas, Texas, ca. mid-1990s

South Dallas, Texas, April 16, 2011

house, Osceola said, "but it was raining too hard and the car wouldn't make it over the muddy roads. So we had to settle for the justice of the peace."

Seven years later, Clarence quit cotton farming because his crops failed. He went to Dallas looking for work and found a job as a janitor and then as a nurse's aide at Parkland Memorial Hospital. The family moved from East Texas to an apartment in South Dallas. Osceola began working in a drugstore on Second Avenue, making sandwiches and serving soft drinks. After about a year she tired of that job and got work as a domestic maid and nanny in the well-to-do households of North Dallas. Clarence left his job at Parkland Hospital to work in the pressing department of a commercial dry cleaning business, where he was employed until ill health forced him to retire in the mid-1970s. Osceola continued to work as a domestic maid and as a visiting nurse but stopped in the mid-1980s because of her husband's illness.

Clarence Mays died November 20, 1985. From then on, Osceola lived alone on a small Social Security income that barely paid the bills, but her faith was strong. She was active in the Good Street Baptist Church, where she was a member of the choir and taught in the Sunday school. In her Bible study classes, she often sang spirituals and recited the poems she had learned from her grandmother and had written when she was a young girl. She participated in the Dallas Folk Festival and in Documentary Arts' Folk Artists in Schools program. In 1989, she became part of the stage show *Texas in Paris,* which toured to the Maison des Cultures du Monde in France and the Centro Flog in Florence, Italy. Osceola Mays died April 20, 2004.

Since Osceola's death, the area around her house has changed. Some of the most rundown houses have been torn down. St. Phillips School on Pennsylvania Avenue, located a few blocks from where Osceola lived, has helped to make the neighborhood safer. In Osceola's church, the tradition of singing spirituals endures.

Howard Dee "Wes" Westmoreland III

Fiddling, Gustine

At the Westmoreland reunion on the banks of the South Leon River near the West Texas town of Gustine (population 457) in Comanche County, fiddle music sets the tone of celebration. Around noon family members begin to arrive in pick-up trucks and cars. Everyone brings a covered dish, whether it's a salad, casserole, barbecue, stew, or fancy dessert. The organizers spread tablecloths on the picnic tables, while others ice down tea and soft drinks or set up folding tables and extra chairs.

Vane Elms, president of the Texas Old Time Fiddlers Association, introduced

Driving to Gustine, Texas, December 21, 2010

me to the Westmoreland family. Her father, Straley Allsup, was a champion fiddler known as the "Fiddling Barber of Gustine." While Elms is not a musician, she loves the music. Listening to her talk about the fiddle contest held annually on a flatbed truck under a circus tent in the center of town, I know I have found the right place to do my fieldwork. I was looking for a family of fiddlers to show how the tradition had changed from dance music to a contest style. The Westmorelands exceed all expectations.

In a shady grove of elm, willow, and sycamore trees, H. D. "Bus" Westmoreland sits across from his grandson Wes, who is a recent graduate of Tarleton State University, and his fourteen-year-old granddaughter Robbin. All three have fiddles, and each takes a turn as the small talk turns to music. Wes calls out "Fort Worth Rag," and Bus starts it off laughing and says, "It's hard to date those tunes because they haven't been written down on paper until now. That's one I got from Major Franklin. When Major couldn't think of a name, he'd call it 'Pig Ankles,' or 'Soap Suds under the Fence,' or whatever popped into his mind at the time. It was just pure chance."

Robbin's dad Gene has one foot up on a stump and plays accompaniment

Wes Westmoreland at age eight,
Fort Worth, Texas, 1970, Courtesy
Westmoreland Family

Gustine, Texas, 198

Wes Westmoreland, Lamkin, Texas, March 1984

(left) Wes Westmoreland with his father "Butch" Westmoreland (guitar) and grandfather H. D. "Bus" Westmoreland, Lamkin, Texas, March 1984

on guitar. In a short time others join in. The musicians are all ages, children under five to adults over eighty.

"It cures what ails you," an elderly woman in a light gingham dress says as she taps the beat with her knitting needle. "It's heart music." "You can feel it," another chimes in. "You can relax and forget everything."

Howard Dee "Wes" Westmoreland III was born September 10, 1962 and grew up in Lamkin, eight miles east of Gustine. As a boy, he says, he heard fiddling "all the time. There's something about it that little kids just like. I loved it. Sunday afternoons with my grandparents were always fun, watching Pa-pa [his grandfather] and my father, my uncles, and cousins all playing together for hours."

As a boy, Wes spent summers at his grandparents' house in Lamkin, and at age nine his grandfather, H. D. "Bus" Westmoreland Sr., began teaching him to play the fiddle in between hunting and fishing trips. "I'd trail him around through the woods and then when we'd get back, we'd sit around the kitchen table and just play. I'd watch where he put his fingers and how he bowed, and I just picked it up." Wes spent countless hours practicing.

Wes Westmoreland's grandfather, H. D. "Bus" Westmoreland Sr., playing at a fiddle contest in Lamesa, Texas, 1960, Courtesy Westmoreland Family

Benny Thomasson and friends, Fort Worth, Texas, 1983

Wes Westmoreland and his father Butch Westmoreland accompanying his grandfather H. D. "Bus" Westmoreland at a fiddle contest, ca. 1978, Courtesy Westmoreland Family

Phiddlin' Pharmacist

Wes Westmoreland, a Temple resident and Scott and White pharmacist, recently won his sixth Texas Fiddling Championship. He learned his musical skills at the knee of his grandfather in Lamkin.

STORY/4D

(left) Newspaper clipping, Courtesy Wes Westmoreland

(right) Wes Westmoreland competing in the 78th Old Fiddlers Contest and Reunion, Athens, Texas, May 28, 2009

When he was frustrated or trying too hard to imitate what he'd just heard, his grandfather would tell him, "If you don't put fire in it, it ain't worth playing."

One day Wes discovered his grandfather's collection of records and started listening to "Texas Shorty" Jim Chancellor and the legendary Benny Thomasson. From his grandfather, Wes learned about contest tunes but also gained a greater understanding of dance music and twin fiddling. In time, Wes started competing in fiddle contests, traveling with his family almost every summer weekend to little towns and festival events, sponsored by the Texas Old Time Fiddlers Association. At the contests, he was often accompanied on guitar by his father, Howard "Butch" Westmoreland, or his uncle, Gene Westmoreland, whose daughter Robbin was also learning from her grandfather and was just beginning to compete.

At age eighteen, Wes went to Weiser, Idaho, where he won the National Junior Championship Fiddle Contest and toyed with the idea of pursuing a career in music. But when he graduated from high school, he enrolled at Tarleton State University in Stephenville to major in Chemistry. While a student, he joined the University Jazz Band and won honors as best soloist on violin. He started playing Western swing dances and shows with Red Steagall and the Coleman County Cowboys. He later met fiddler Randy Elmore. "Randy and I would talk about music theory and harmony parts," he says, "and he helped

Lamkin, Texas, December 21, 2010

Wes Westmoreland tuning his fiddle in the living room of his parents' house, Lamkin, Texas, December 21, 2010

Wes Westmoreland with his father Butch Westmoreland, uncle Gene Westmoreland, and son Tanner Westmoreland, Lamkin, Texas, December 21, 2010

me to find the 'five-string fiddle' that I've played ever since. Randy was a big influence."

After graduating from Tarleton State University, Wes got a job playing with Boxcar Willie in Branson, Missouri. The following year, Mel Tillis hired him to play in his band. With Tillis, Wes toured extensively, appearing on television broadcasts such as *Nashville Now* and *Austin City Limits* and performing at the Grand Ole Opry and other showplaces across the country. While Wes still liked playing the traditional tunes he had learned growing up, the music he performed with Mel Tillis was significantly different. "It was commercial country," Wes says. "I was just a sideman in the band." Wes enjoyed his career as a professional musician, but after fourteen years on the road, he decided to return to school because he wanted to spend more time with his children. He attended the University of Houston College of Pharmacy from 1999 to 2003. After finishing his degree, he moved to Temple, where he accepted a residency at Scott and White Hospital and then joined the staff as a patient care pharmacist.

Today, Wes is still active as a fiddler, performing in fiddle contests around the state and working as a judge and teacher in his spare time. His awards include National Junior Champ 1980 (Wieser, Idaho); Texas Old Time Fiddlers Association (TOTFA) State Champion 1985, 1986, 2002 (Nacogdoches, Waco,

Main Street, Gustine, Texas, December 21, 2011

and Killeen, Texas); World Champion 1985, 1987, 2003 (Crockett, Texas); and Texas State Champion 1988, 2001–2004 (Halletsville).

Music is an integral part of Wes's life and family. His daughter Katherine sings and plays the flute, and his son Tanner is carrying on the family tradition of fiddling. The Westmoreland family has six generations of fiddlers. While the tunes have been passed on from one generation to the next, each has added its own interpretation, influenced not only by family members but also by other fiddlers around the state.

Over the years Texas fiddling has evolved from a highly rhythmic, fast-paced dance style to slow-tempo contest music, often performed with innovative variations and embellishment. Benny Thomasson and his contemporaries Major Franklin and the Solomon brothers, Irvin and Norman, are often credited with introducing in the 1950s and 1960s what is today called the "Texas-style." Texas-style fiddlers, like Wes Westmoreland, Jim Chancellor, and Valerie Morris, often use fairly long bow strokes that are executed smoothly with the bow rarely leaving the strings and with the number of notes played on each stroke varying from a single note to seven or eight.

In fiddle contests across Texas, judges encourage personal expression and improvisation to create, as the Texas Old Time Fiddlers Association states on its website, "richly melodic and pleasingly complicated sounds that are free of monotony and repetition." However, in performance, the original melody line of the tune must be identifiable. Wes says, "Playing in tune with good rhythm is always necessary when it comes to a contest; however, it's not the only thing a tune requires. 'Top shelf' tunes to me are not necessarily those played completely 'perfect.' A perfect tune without life or that spark doesn't grab me as much. There is a certain groove/timing/rhythm that—when hit just right—really makes the tune come alive. I look for that groove a lot. I'm always open to new ways to turn a phrase, and really look for it when judging a tune, as long as it remains true to the melody. My playing tastes have always leaned toward Texas-style breakdowns, Western swing, and jazz violin, mostly because that's what I grew up hearing, but I am very open and appreciative of all styles. The best advice I can give is to play songs you like and enjoy playing. Have fun with it. Remember: songs are stories, not just a bunch of notes. Some, like 'Sally Gooden,' are about people, and when I'm playing I'm thinking about the story of the song, even if I don't know all the lyrics.

Straley Allsup (remembered as "The Fiddling Barber of Gustine"), Gustine, Texas, December 21, 2011

Picturing the story helps with the dynamics of what I'm playing. 'Tom and Jerry' and 'Dusty Miller' are about horses; 'Forked Creek' is a place. When I'm listening, I want to feel like I've been there, like I've heard something new, even if I already know the tune. Louis Franklin used to say, 'If everything is right, your fiddle is singing the song.'"

Miguel Pedraza Sr.

Tigua Drumming and Chanting, El Paso

The early morning sun shimmers through the jagged fibers and fleshy leaves of the lechugilla plants scattered in clumps across the Chihuahuan desert about fourteen miles southeast of downtown El Paso. The air is cool and dry and the sky turquoise blue as I turn onto the dusty road leading to Barrio de Los Indios on the Tigua Indian Reservation, located at Ysleta del Sur Pueblo.

Miguel Pedraza Sr. steps from his small adobe house to greet me, his hand

Driving through El Paso, Texas to Ysleta del Sur Pueblo, April 15, 2011

Entrance to Ysleta del Sur Pueblo, El Paso, Texas, April 15, 2011

extended in a welcoming gesture. His eyes are warm but probing. He explains that he has lived on this land of his ancestors for his entire life, but instead of answering my questions, he wants to know more about me.

"You believe in something?"

"A higher being," I reply softly.

"You don't believe in something very strong, do you?"

"Yes, I do," I answer more assertively.

"What?"

"Nature."

"You believe in nature?

"The creator of nature."

"Now I'm understanding you," he says with compassion. "Just like you, I believe in nature. I believe in the sun. I believe in the moon. See, that's what makes me strong. In other words, that's spiritual. We live by the food we take, water, fresh air, nature. You can see nature on every little living thing. You believe in something that is the real truth—nature."

The house where Miguel Pedraza lived,
Ysleta del Sur Pueblo, El Paso, Texas,
April 15, 2011

Miguel Pedraza, Ysleta del Sur Pueblo,
El Paso, Texas, January 7, 1987

Pedraza motions me to follow him inside and to take a seat on the couch in his living room. A hand-woven Indian blanket covers the tattered cushions. He lifts his drum from the corner of the room and beats a steady rhythm with a stick covered in deer hide as he begins to chant.

M IGUEL PEDRAZA SR. was born June 30, 1904, in Barrio de los Indios, an enclave of Tigua Indians living in small adobe houses, many of which had no plumbing or electricity. When Miguel was a child, his father, Luz Pedraza, was killed in a gun battle with Texas Rangers. After his father's death, Miguel was raised by his mother and Benselado Granillo, who had worked for the US Calvary as an Indian scout in the 1880s. Miguel's memories of his father were sketchy, although he did recall standing at his side at tribal ceremonies and learning to play the ceremonial drum and chant in the Tigua and Piro languages.

The modern Tigua of Ysleta del Sur are descendants of the Tiwa, Piro, and Towa Indians, who lived in pueblos along the Rio Grande and fled the Pueblo Revolt of 1680, an uprising against Spanish colonization of the Americas in the New Spain province of New Mexico. They called themselves "Tigua" (after the Spanish spelling of their name) because the majority of the refugees were from the Tiwa Pueblo of Isleta, located near Albuquerque. When they settled southeast of present-day El Paso, they christened their village Ysleta del Sur (Isleta of the South).

Like many Native Americans, the Tigua accepted the Catholicism forced upon them by Spanish missionaries, but in their practices, they often rejected orthodox rituals in an effort to preserve their time-honored customs and beliefs, especially as they related to the importance of nature. The traditional chants that Pedraza performed were associated with both tribal ceremonies and Christian holidays, such as Christmas and the Fiesta de San Antonio, which is the principal public celebration, held annually on June 13 at the Ysleta del Sur Pueblo. "The fiesta starts in the morning at the kiva, our ceremonial structure," Tigua Tribal Historian and Preservation Officer Javier Loera says. "Then there is a Mass at the Ysleta Mission Church, followed by traditional ceremonial and social dances."

Isleta Pueblo, New Mexico (old adobe home in foreground), 1965, Photograph by Tom Diamond, Courtesy Ysleta del Sur Pueblo

Piro Drum of Senecu del Sur, eight-pointed star design, ca. 1960s, Photograph by Tom Diamond, Courtesy Ysleta del Sur Pueblo

Miguel Pedraza, Ysleta del Sur Pueblo, El Paso, Texas, January 7, 1987

Fiesta de San Antonio, Ysleta del Sur Pueblo, June 13, 1965, Photograph by Tom Diamond, Courtesy Ysleta del Sur Pueblo

Miguel Pedraza on Ysleta del Sur Pueblo brochure cover, El Paso, Texas, ca. 1980s, Courtesy Yselta del Sur Pueblo

Celebrants in front of La Misión de Corpus Christi de San Antonio de la Ysleta del Sur, June 13, 1898, Courtesy Arizona State Museum and Ysleta del Sur Pueblo

Loera, born in 1955, learned the Tigua language as a child from his grandparents and from Miguel Pedraza, who was highly regarded as a drummer and singer of traditional chants. "Dating these chants," Loera maintains, "is difficult. We don't measure them in years. For us, they are as old as time, passed on orally from one generation to the next. Through the chants we preserve our customs and our language. The Tigua language was on the verge of being lost, but we've been teaching it in classes to our children since the late 1980s."

"As far as I know, the women," Pedraza said in the 1980s, "never chant or sing together with the men. They know songs, but they're different. From my mother, I learned the Tiwa language, and in the songs, I use individual Tigua words, but not in all songs. Some chants are only sounds."

During Tigua ceremonies, a group of men stand in a circle around the drum, which is played by the War Captain, elected for life by the tribe. Usually, Pedraza explained, the War Captain starts the drumming, using a single drumstick, often made from willow or mesquite that is wrapped at one end with wool and then covered with deer hide. "The War Captain leads the chant and everyone else follows," Pedraza said. "Each chant has a different rhythm,

Interior of the house of José Granillo, Tribal Cacique (Barrio de los Indios), 1965, Photograph by Tom Diamond, Courtesy Ysleta del Sur Pueblo

Javier Loera, Tribal Historian, Ysleta del
Sur Pueblo, El Paso, Texas, April 15, 2011

and after the first three or four songs, the War Captain sometimes hands off the drumstick to a younger member of the tribe. The War Captain gives him permission to play. In this way, the young ones can learn, and the tradition continues."

Pedraza believed his drum, hand-crafted from cottonwood and buffalo hide, was over three hundred years old and was brought by the Tigua to this region of the Rio Grande around 1682, when the Ysleta del Sur Pueblo was established. "The face on the drum is the moon face," he pointed out. "We use this side for nighttime. And the other side, we use it for daytime, the sun. Who painted the drum? I don't know. I cannot answer that. It was painted when I got it."

Ysleta del Sur Pueblo, El Paso, Texas,
April 15, 2011

Ysleta del Sur Pueblo, El Paso, Texas, April 15, 2011

Leaving Ysleta del Sur Pueblo, El Paso, Texas, April 15, 2011

Pedraza married Margarita Quintañilla, a Mexican American, in 1938. They had one son, Miguel Pedraza Jr., who, like his father, was actively involved in Tigua tribal affairs. Over the years, Miguel Sr. worked as a farmer, maintenance man, and bus driver for the Ysleta Independent School District, but he was always a tireless volunteer working for the advancement of his people. In the 1960s, Pedraza met with Governor Abieta of the New Mexico Tiguas and with Tom Diamond, an El Paso attorney and the local Democratic Party chairman, who, in turn, brought him to the attention of US Senator Ralph R. Yarborough and Governor John Connally. Together, they succeeded in gaining the state's recognition of the Tiguas in 1967. The following year, Pedraza and Diamond appealed to the US Congress. On the floor of the House of Representatives, Pedraza pleaded, "What I ask you is to give my people back their water. They have no water." In the end, his fight was successful, although it was not until 1987 that President Ronald Reagan signed the Ysleta del Sur Restoration Act, making the Tiguas eligible for various federal benefits. Pedraza was elected governor of the Tiguas in 1971 and 1972 and served as a tribal elder, mentor, and teacher until his death on April 24, 1988. His chants live on, and continue to be taught to children in the Tigua education classes and performed in tribal ceremonies.

Miguel Pedraza Jr., Socorro, Texas, April 15, 2011

Socorro, Texas, twenty miles east of El
Paso, April 15, 2011

Alexander H. Moore

Barrelhouse Blues, Dallas

On Tuesday afternoon at the Martin Luther King Jr. Center in South Dallas, Alex Moore holds court. A group of elderly African American men gathers around him, laughing loudly at his stories and jokes, before they move into the activity room to play dominoes. Four of the men sit in metal folding chairs on each side of a small square table, and the others cluster around the perimeter. Moore

Driving to South Dallas, Texas, May 2, 2011

The Martin Luther King Jr. Complex, Dallas, Texas, April 16, 2011

studies the other players, trying to anticipate their next move. When he scores a point, he slaps his black and white domino tile onto the table and roars.

The game over, Moore stands up slowly and ambles over to the upright piano in the corner of room. He lowers himself slowly into his chair and scoots forward; his long bony fingers improvise a melody but then pounce on the piano keys in a loud crescendo. Conversations stop, and everyone is poised to listen. The notes of his piano blues rush forward in a fluid run and then dip down in intensity as he sings with a throaty voice.

Moore loves having an audience, and my presence in the room seems to energize him, even though the other senior citizens aren't sure what to make of me. I do my best to show respect to the people around me and only photograph those who consent. If someone waves me away, I focus in another direction. Just about everyone at the Martin Luther King Jr. Recreation Center knows that Moore is a celebrity of sorts who frequently performs in nightclubs around Dallas. "We're used to people coming around here looking for ole Alex," one man says to me as I walk past the table where he's playing cards. "They can't get enough of him."

Alexander H. Moore playing dominoes, Martin Luther King Jr. Recreation Center, Dallas, Texas, 1984

Alexander Herman Moore was born November 22, 1899, in an area of Dallas known as Freedmantown, where emancipated slaves were given a place to live. During Reconstruction, African Americans built a thriving community with schools, churches, cafes, and other small businesses. But life was hard. Racism and discrimination made it extremely difficult to find good jobs. Blues music answered a need for a release from the pressures of everyday life.

The blues is intensely personal music that originated among the first generation of African Americans born out of slavery. It identifies itself with the feelings of the listener—suffering, hope, economic failure, the breakup of families, and the desire to escape reality by traveling and relocating. With its emphasis on the experience of the individual and his or her successes and trials, blues reflects Western concepts. Yet, as a musical form, the blues shows little Western influence. The traditional three-line, twelve-bar, A-A-B verse form of the blues arises from no apparent Western source, although some blues does incorporate Anglo-American ballad forms, which have six-, ten-, or sixteen-bar structures. Early blues drew on the sources available at the time of its creation: field hollers and shouts, which it most closely resembles melodically; songster ballads, from which it borrowed some imagery and guitar patterns; and church music, which trained the voices and ears of black children. These, with the exception of the ballad, were the descendants of African percussive rhythms, syncopation, and call-and-response singing.

The first blues that Moore heard was at his cousin's house around 1906 when he was six or seven years old. "He played piano while I was playing marbles," he said. "They danced and sang while he played the piano."

Moore taught himself to play the piano in white people's homes where he delivered groceries as a boy. "Every time I'd walk by, I'd pluck one note," he said, "and every day it would be a different note. That's the way I learned to play the piano." As he got older, he heard black piano players at house parties who performed a distinctive style of blues that brought together elements of boogie-woogie with ragtime and stride.

Characteristic of boogie-woogie is the use of recurring bass patterns that lay the foundation rhythmically and harmonically for short melodic passages. Similarly, ragtime and stride piano depend on repetitive bass patterns, though the rhythms are often broken and include more complex harmonies. Together,

South Dallas, Texas, April 16, 2011

Alexander H. Moore, Dallas, Texas, 1938, Courtesy Alexander H. Moore

these styles encourage spontaneity and improvisation in performance. It was a music that in Texas was called "barrelhouse blues" because it was often played in a shed or makeshift building where drinks were served on a long slab of wood mounted on top of two or three fifty-five-gallon barrels.

Growing up, Moore was never able to support himself playing the piano. He worked a variety of jobs, including dishwashing, driving mules to haul gravel, and serving as a custodian and hotel porter. Piano playing was a way to earn a little bit extra, but the people who came to house parties often only paid a nickel or a dime, and sometimes the owner of the house might give him a tip. House parties were held in someone's home, usually in the living room with the furniture moved aside or piled up in a back room.

Moore's music became popular among people in his community, and in 1929 a scout for Columbia Records invited him to travel to Chicago, where he recorded six songs, including "Blue Boomer Blues," "Ice Pick Blues," and "West Texas Woman." He got the nickname "Whistling Alex Moore" because he liked to whistle to open a song or to accompany himself when he was playing the piano. But his first recordings did not sell very well, and he was unable to get his music issued again until 1937. Once again, not many people bought his records. He did, however, record eight more songs in 1947 and four in 1951.

In 1960 blues researchers Paul Oliver and Chris Strachwitz found him on the screened porch of a small North Dallas bar. He didn't have a piano, but he took them to the home of Madame Pratt, a piano teacher who lived nearby. The recordings Moore made on that day introduced a white audience to his music. Soon he was invited to perform at festivals in the United States and to tour Europe as part of the American Folk Blues Festival. In 1987, he was awarded a National Heritage Fellowship by the National Endowment for the Arts for excellence in folk and traditional arts. Moore was an exemplary performer, actively involved in the preservation and perpetuation of traditional barrelhouse blues.

From the late 1960s until his death in 1989, he performed often at festivals and nightclubs, where his audiences were predominantly white. He also continued to play at the Martin Luther King Jr. Center. Moore had an upright piano in his small apartment in the Oak Cliff area of Dallas, but he rarely practiced, though he sometimes gave pointers to aspiring blues pianists, both black and white musicians, who admired his style of performance. By the end of his life, his songs became less structured. He often rambled about his

Alexander H. Moore (dishwasher) playing at the Southern House ("White Patrons Only"),
Dallas, Texas, 1947, Courtesy Alexander H. Moore

Alexander H. Moore, Oak Cliff, Texas, 1988

experiences growing up in a kind of talking blues. He loved telling stories through his music, mixing details of his own life with piano sounds that changed with his mood. With his left hand, the bass might be steady, while the right hand wandered on the keys. There was a call and response between his singing and the piano. The tone was sometimes soft and slow, sometimes thunderous and fast. He liked to say he never knew exactly what he was going to play until he played it. "The music is always here when I get ready," Moore laughed. "The piano kind of plays itself. I've always said that if I don't improve every night, then you don't owe me anything, but they always paid me."

Alex Moore, Sr.
"Blues Artist"
3140 Garden Lane
Dallas, TX 75215

Alexander H. Moore at the Chicago
Blues Festival, 1985, Courtesy
Alexander H. Moore

South Dallas, April 16, 2011

South Dallas, April 16, 2011

Barrelhouse Blues, Dallas \ 71

Since Alex Moore's death, the style of barrelhouse piano that he played lives on in a new form and is often integrated into contemporary blues and jazz. The concert halls and nightclubs in which Moore performed in the last decades of his life have become the mainstay of his style of music. At the Meyerson Symphony Center in the Dallas Arts District, the Dress Circle Stairway named in his honor overlooks the area of Freedmantown where he grew up and spent most of his life.

W. W. "Skinny" Trammell

Guitar Maker and Musician, Lone Star

When I stop for gas in Lone Star about six miles south of Daingerfield on US Highway 259, deep in the Piney Woods of Northeast Texas, a white-haired man chewing tobacco exits his small storefront wearing a red and white ball cap with the brim flipped up. As I roll down the window, he motions for me to stay inside and says proudly, "We're a full-service station." Then he points to the two

Leaving Dallas, Texas, May 2, 2011

W. W. "Skinny" Trammell's Fina Station,
Lone Star, Texas, October 27, 1987

pumps, "Unleaded or premium?" I tell him "unleaded" and that I need to use the restroom. He shows me the way. When I return he's finished checking the oil and is washing the windshield with a squeegee and cotton rag. I thank him and follow him back inside to pay and am completely surprised. There are wood-chips scattered on the floor. Guitars, fiddles, and mandolins in different stages of construction are on the shelves and stacked in the corner.

The conversation shifts to music and instrument making. He introduces himself: "The name's Trammell, Skinny Trammell." Before long, we're sitting side by side in his office. I've taken my tape recorder from the trunk of my car and I have a microphone in my hand. I ask if I can buy a bottle of water, and he looks up with a little grin. "Help yourself. There's a fresh paper cup by the water cooler." A light autumn breeze wafts through the open door, and as the after-noon turns to dusk there are few interruptions. Lone Star has a population of about 1,600 people, and Trammell explains that most of his customers come in the early morning or on their way home from work.

WINFORD WORKMAN TRAMMELL, or W. W. as he prefers to be called, was named for the physician who delivered him on January 31, 1929, in Balfora, a small town in Wise County in Northwest Texas. He was one of fourteen children. Trammell's parents eked out a living during the Great Depression as sharecroppers. "We did stock farming," he says, "and raising cotton and mostly everything we ate— green beans, corn, watermelon, cantaloupe, you name it." His brother, who was twenty years old when Trammell was born, gave him the nickname "Skinny" when he was just a baby. "I was the thirteenth of fourteen children. My brother was working for the WPA [Works Progress Administration] and they asked him to list all the members in his family and he couldn't remember my name. So, he wrote 'Skinny Flint' and it just stuck."

Trammell's interest in music started early. "We had a Victrola," he recalls. "It was a console that stood up about four feet high. I had to get up in a chair to put the record on to play it. Oh, we had Carter Family records, Jimmie Rodgers, and Gid Tanner and the Skillet Lickers—that's the old fiddle tunes and what have you, back in the old days. It was the high point of my day," Trammell says. "We had long days on the farm."

"Skinny" Trammell working on the neck of one of his handcrafted guitars in his Fina station, Lone Star, Texas, October 27, 1987

"Skinny" Trammell's office and instrument-making workshop inside his Fina station, Lone Star, Texas, October 27, 1987

As a child, Trammell attended a one-room schoolhouse. "I only went through the eighth grade," he says. "I had to go to work. I hardly had any money to buy clothes. I just stayed on the farm and helped daddy do what needed to be done." When he was thirteen years old, he wanted to buy a guitar, but he couldn't afford it. Two of his brothers chipped in to buy him one for $15, and he learned to play. Two years later, after his family moved to Paradise, Texas, about forty miles north of Fort Worth, Trammell started his own band called the Country Balladeers. "Mostly, we played Western swing—the music of Bob Wills and Ernest Tubb. We played around Fort Worth, at places like the Cowtown Roundup. On Friday nights, they would tape it, and we could hear it on the radio on Saturday morning. That was in the middle forties, around

1946 or 1947. I had my nephew, Travis West, he played steel guitar. And a boy from Chico, August Long, he played fiddle. Another boy played rhythm guitar, Leland Carruthers. And I played guitar and sang, or tried to."

Trammell started making his own instruments in the 1960s around the time he began to lose interest in commercial country music. "It was becoming too electric, too loud," he says. "I liked acoustic music. I met a boy named R. A. Davis, who had moved to Lone Star from North Carolina, and we started playing together. I played guitar mostly, a little fiddle, and he played guitar and banjo. So, I started going to bluegrass festivals and fiddle contests. One day, I met a guy from Garland in Gilmer at the old time fiddlers' contest. He had a couple fiddles that he'd made. Well, I've always whittled a little all my life, and carved, and I thought, well, I believe I can make one that good, maybe better. So, I didn't know where to start. And I finally got everything together. And the first one I made, I had it about half done, and nothing would fit. I slammed it across a corner of the building and busted it all to pieces. Started over. Never had a problem since, and the only thing I've ever been told about how to build an instrument was how to bend that wood to the shape of the sides. I learned it all by experiment."

"Skinny" Trammell's instrument-making tools inside his Fina station, Lone Star, Texas, October 27, 1987

Guitar Maker and Musician, Lone Star \ 77

"Skinny" Trammell sizing the back of one his handcrafted guitars inside his Fina station, Lone Star, Texas, October 27, 1987

"Skinny" Trammell's tools inside his Fina station, Lone Star, Texas, October 27, 1987

"Skinny" Trammell's tools and guitar parts inside his Fina station, Lone Star, Texas, October 27, 1987

Over the years, Trammell says he's made about fifty-eight guitars, fifty-seven fiddles, twenty mandolins, ten dobros (resonator guitars), and two ukuleles, all constructed in his spare time. To support his family, he worked as a trucker for most of his adult life, a profession that gave him the opportunity to travel and find some unexpected sources of wood for his instrument making. "I hauled oil pipe out of here for twenty-seven years. I'd go into Houston, San Antone, some places like that, and I'd go to lumberyards and sawmills and pick up wood. Walnut, rosewood. I've got walnut I've had forty years. And it was old when I got it. A guy gave me a fireplace mantel made out of walnut. It's probably a hundred years old. It's put together with square nails. And one of my friends from Bridgeport gave me an old homemade trunk made out of walnut, and it was put together with square nails. And I made two fiddles out of that. They turned out real good."

Trammell says the prices of his instruments vary. "The most I've got for a fiddle is $2,500; for a guitar, $2,000. And mandolins, about $1,500; dobros, about $1,500 to $2,000. But I was never just in it for the money. I enjoy making them, and I like the music."

Most people find out about Trammel's instruments by word of mouth from

One of "Skinny" Trammell's handcrafted guitar tops inside his Fina station, Lone Star, Texas, October 27, 1987

"Skinny" Trammell fitting the top of one his handcrafted guitars in his Fina station, Lone Star, Texas, October 27, 1987

Skinny" Trammell fitting the top of one of his handcrafted guitars in his Fina station, Lone Star, Texas, October 27, 1987

"Skinny" Trammell fitting the neck of one of his handcrafted guitars in his Fina station, Lone Star, Texas, October 27, 1987

"Skinny" Trammell sitting in front of his Fina Station, Lone Star, Texas, October 27, 1986

musicians who own one. "I'd bring them to jam sessions, where folks could try them out, and sometimes someone would buy one. But in my home county, in forty-four years, I've only sold five instruments, fiddles, guitars, mandolins, whatever. There hasn't been anybody around here to back me. I've sold several guitars in Florida, California, Virginia, Tennessee, Oklahoma, Arkansas, Louisiana—everywhere but here. They haven't supported me much."

While the lack of local interest in buying his instruments is frustrating, Trammell still loves to play music for family and friends. "We've had a bluegrass show for the last twenty years here in Lone Star in an old army barracks. It was started by a man named Curtis Roundtree . . . it's called the Pickin' Place. We have it the second Saturday every month. We get anywhere from about a hundred to five hundred people. And that's about the only place I play anymore. But I don't play there much. A lot of the ones I used to play with, they've done gone. But there are others, the young ones, carrying it on."

Lydia Mendoza

Boleros, Corridos, *and* Rancheras, *Houston*

At the 1986 Dallas Folk Festival, Lydia Mendoza takes the stage with grace. In her frilly white dress trimmed in red, a theatrical adaptation of the traditional Adelita costume, she is indeed *La Alondra de la Frontera* (The Meadowlark of the Border), as she was known at the height of her career. Her thick black hair, pulled back with a long barrette, belies her age. She lifts her twelve-string guitar high against her breast and begins to play, singing one of her favorites, "Acércane a Tu Vida" ("Bring Me into Your Life"). Her voice soars above the chords she strums and the melodies she picks with her bare fingers, using her signature thumb-brush and arpeggio styles.

Driving to San Antonio, Texas, May 7, 2011, Photograph by Alan Govenar

Lydia Mendoza singing in front of her house, Houston, Texas, March 15, 1987

Mendoza's husband Fred Martínez stands in the wings and radiates a deep pride. Over the years, Martínez has been devoted to his wife's career, traveling with her to performance dates and catering to her needs. Mendoza moves with measured steps and an air of elegance that brings rousing applause from the thousands of people who have crowded in front of the outdoor stage at City Hall Plaza for her performance.

Next to me in the front row is Chris Strachwitz, who founded Arhoolie Records in 1960 to record American roots music. Strachwitz is especially fond of Mendoza and has traveled from El Cerrito, California to see her along with Alex Moore and others he has recorded over the years. Sitting nearby are Valerio Longoria and Narciso Martínez, two legends in the development of conjunto norteño music, who had performed earlier in the day. I'm taking a much-needed break. Directing the Dallas Folk Festival is all consuming, involving the management of every step in the process, from research, fieldwork, programming, and staging to making arrangements for travel, lodging, and food and meeting the needs of craft demonstrators, sound engineers, lighting technicians, concessionaires, and the people of all ages in attendance.

Not long after the festival, I travel to Houston to do a follow-up interview with Mendoza for the *Traditional Music in Texas* radio series. At her home in Houston, Mendoza likes to stay busy, even when she's not touring and recording. She tells me in Spanish, with her husband acting as translator, that she enjoys the "simple pleasures" of household chores and sewing. "I make my own costumes for my performance work," she says. "I make the flowers, and then I sew the dresses. I rarely buy a ready-made dress or outfit. I like to make my outfits, my dresses, my housedresses, everything. So, there's always something to do at home."

Alazan-Apache Courts, a public housing project built between 1939 and 1942, where Lydia Mendoza and her family lived. Today, the homes have been renovated. An exhibition of photographs depicting day-to-day life during the 1940s and 1950s has been installed on the surrounding fences. San Antonio, Texas, May 6, 2011, Photograph by Alan Govenar

The Guadalupe Theatre, located at 1301 Guadalupe Street, was built in 1942 and was the anchor to a thriving entertainment district that featured circus performers, singers, stage actors, comedians, and other vaudeville performers, including Lydia Mendoza. The theatre was restored and reopened in 1984. Today it is a multicultural nonprofit organization dedicated to the preservation and presentation of the arts and culture of Mexican American, Latino, and Native American people. San Antonio, Texas, May 6, 2010, Photograph by Alan Govenar

LYDIA MENDOZA was born May 13, 1916, in Houston, Texas. Her father worked as a mechanic on the rail line that linked Laredo, Texas with Monterrey, Nuevo León, Mexico. He was assigned to work both sides of the border and usually took his family with him. Lydia did not attend school as a young girl, but her mother, Leonor, taught her and the other children to read at home. At the age of four, Lydia became interested in music: "We came to a little town in Texas called Ennis. We lived there for a little while, and it was exactly there that I began to feel the impulse of the music. . . . My mother would take out a guitar and play whenever she got a chance . . . she had an exceptionally pretty voice. . . . I was four years old, and I wanted to play the guitar, so much that I tried to get hold of my mother's guitar. But she never allowed me to touch it . . . and to prevent me from getting at it, she put a nail up real high and hung it up so that I couldn't reach it. One time when she was in the kitchen, I grabbed a chair and climbed up and took down the guitar very carefully. Then when I was back down on the floor, I sat down and started to play it with just one finger. As soon as my mother heard that sound she burst out of the kitchen and told me that if I ever took the guitar down again, she was

Lydia Mendoza recording at home, 1938, Courtesy University of Texas, The Institute of Texan Cultures, San Antonio Light Collection

The Mendoza family variety show, featuring Francisca ("Panchita") Mendoza (top left), Maria Mendoza (top right), Leonor Zamarripa Mendoza (seated), Juanita Mendoza (lower left), and Manuel Mendoza (lower right), 1935, Courtesy Houston Metropolitan Research Center, Houston Public Library

going to punish me severely. Well, she put the fear of God in me, and I never did it again. I would just stand in front of where it was hanging and stare at that guitar."

"One day when I was playing outside," Mendoza told Chris Strachwitz and researcher James Nicolopulos, "there were some little neighbor girls playing with some of those little rubber bands. They put them in their mouth and stretched

Lydia Mendoza recording at Texas Hotel with Eli Oberstein supervising, San Antonio, Texas, October 1936, Courtesy San Antonio Light Collection, U.T. Institute of Texan Cultures

them to make a musical sound. So, I said to myself, 'I'm going to make a guitar.' I went into the patio of the house, and I found a little plank of wood. I remembered that Papá had a little can full of nails in the kitchen, and I went and got six small ones. I pounded them into the board—three on each end. And I said, 'Well, here is my guitar.' But the strings were still lacking. So I asked my little friend if she would give me some of those rubber bands she had.

"'Yes, my papa has plenty, and I brought a whole bunch,' she said.

"'I only want three,' I replied.

"So, I hooked up the rubber bands from one end of the board to the other. And, of course, with pressure they made a sound, which for me was the sound of a guitar. And it made me so happy to imagine at that age that I had a guitar. It was a guitar for me . . . that was the first toy I made for myself. And I just imitated the way that I saw my mother play her guitar."

Finally, when Lydia was seven, her mother taught her to play a real guitar, and it wasn't long before she, in turn, began teaching her sister Maria. Lydia also took up mandolin and violin. The Mendozas formed a family band and by the late 1920s were entertaining Mexican and Mexican American workers in

Lydia Mendoza singing and playing guitar with mariachis, 1985, Photograph by Chris Strachwitz, Courtesy Arhoolie Records

Lydia Mendoza with Fred Martinez, Denver, Colorado, ca. 1960s, Courtesy Yolanda Hernandez

Lydia Mendoza's daughter Yolanda Hernandez in her living room, San Antonio, Texas, May 6, 2011

Lydia Mendoza with her daughter, Yolanda Hernandez, San Antonio, Texas, ca. 1980s, Courtesy Yolanda Hernandez

Yard shrine in front of the house of Lydia Mendoza's daughter, Yolanda Hernandez, San Antonio, Texas, May 6, 2011

restaurants and barbershops in Texas's Lower Rio Grande Valley. Lydia Mendoza said, "Papá would go in and ask permission to play, and then, if folks were there, we'd sit down and sing, and people would give us tips. And later on, when harvesting season came along, we'd go to the little town where the workers were, where there would be gatherings of Mexican people. We'd sing there and get some pocket money." The family often hitchhiked from one community to the next since they did not own a car.

In 1928, the family saw an announcement in *La Prensa,* a popular newspaper in South Texas, which said the OKeh record label was looking for singers to record. They borrowed a friend's car and made the trip to San Antonio, where a representative from OKeh Records brought them into a studio. "We were told through an interpreter that they were going to give us $140 for twenty songs—but in the end, we only recorded eleven," Mendoza recalled. "We performed traditional Mexican songs, like 'Monterrey,' 'Las Cuatro Milpas,' and "Cancion de Amor.'"

After the recording session, the family moved to Detroit, where they worked as professional musicians for over a year. In Detroit they found receptive audiences among Mexican Americans who had migrated north to work in the automobile industry. In 1930, along with scores of other Mexican workers, the Mendoza family headed back south. They stopped in Houston, where they had family and friends. The family continued to entertain within the city's Mexican communities, notably at Magnolia Park, a subdivision a few miles east of Houston. The Mendozas moved to San Antonio in 1932, when Lydia was sixteen. It was in San Antonio that she began playing the *guitarra doble,* the twelve-string guitar, which she adapted to better accompany her singing style. She tuned it in the key of B to create a pitch that was halfway between a standard twelve-string guitar and a *bajo sexto.* Mendoza's guitar playing had a booming bass sound that complemented the expressiveness of her voice.

For two years, beginning around 1934, the Mendozas struggled to earn their living playing at San Antonio's open-air market, Plaza del Zacate. By this time Lydia was singing solo. After hearing her sing with her family, Manuel J. Cortez, a local radio announcer, invited her to sing on his thirty-minute program, *La Voz Latina.* She won the program's amateur competition. Her radio debut made her so popular that Cortez asked her family to allow her to be a regular on the radio. He secured a commercial sponsor willing to pay her $3.50

a week for her radio performances, and her parents agreed. Meanwhile, the family continued to sing in area restaurants. In 1934, Lydia made her first solo recordings for Bluebird Records. Her first record to be released was *Mal Hombre* ("Evil Man"), whose lyrics she had seen on a chewing-gum wrapper. The record was so successful that Bluebird offered her a contract and continued to record her over the next ten years.

In 1935, Lydia married Juan Alvarado, a cobbler, who helped to support her career. They had three daughters, Lydia, Yolanda, and Maria Leonor, whom she tried to teach to play the guitar. "She wanted to give us the opportunity," Yolanda recalls, "but we didn't follow through."

During the late 1930s and early 1940s, when Lydia wasn't recording, she continued to tour with her family throughout the Southwest, playing in parish halls and theaters for predominantly Mexican American audiences. By this time the Mendoza family owned an automobile. They were able to travel greater distances with considerably less stress. After Lydia's mother died in the early 1950s, she began touring as a soloist, accompanied only by her twelve-

Flower stand, South General McMullen Drive, San Antonio, Texas, May 6, 2011

string guitar, but when her husband died in 1961, she became deeply depressed and lost interest in performing. In 1964, she remarried, and her second husband, Fred Martínez, also a shoemaker, helped to revitalize her career. Despite arthritis in her hands, she continued to perform until the late 1980s, when a stroke left her partially paralyzed.

Mendoza received many honors over the course of her long career, during which she became known as *"La Alondra de la Frontera"* ("The Meadowlark of the Border") and *"La Cancionera de los Pobres"* ("The Songstress of the Poor"). She recorded over two hundred songs on more than fifty albums for labels including RCA, Columbia, Azteca, Peerless, El Zarape, and Discos Falcon. Stylistically, she was most well known for her deeply emotional *ranchera* songs. Even when she sang *boleros* (slow-tempo dance songs) and *corridos* (ballads), she often did so in the *ranchera* style. Traditional *rancheras* are often sung by one

Flower stand, South General McMullen Drive, San Antonio, Texas, May 6, 2011

San Fernando Cemetery #2, where Lydia Mendoza is buried, San Antonio, Texas, May 6, 2011

person with a guitar and are usually about love, patriotism, or nature, consisting of an instrumental introduction, verse, and refrain. Mendoza in her singing of *rancheras* had great emotive power, not only in her resonant voice but also in the *gritos* (high-pitched screams) that punctuated her songs.

In 1982, Mendoza was awarded a National Heritage Fellowship from the National Endowment for the Arts. In 1984, she was inducted into the Tejano Music Hall of Fame, and in 1991, into the Conjunto Music Hall of Fame. In 1999, she was awarded the National Medal of Arts, and in 2003 she was a recipient of the Texas Cultural Trust's Texas Medal of Arts. Lydia Mendoza died December 20, 2007.

Looking back, Lydia's daughter, Yolanda Hernandez, has some regrets that she didn't try harder to learn her mother's music. "My sisters and I never learned," she says, "and none of our children ever had any interest. But my mother did teach Blanca Rosa, when she was about fourteen or fifteen years old. Blanca is a couple of years older than me and she's still performing today, not so much on the guitar, but she is still singing. Now, the youngest of my grandchildren, my daughter's son, the three-year-old, he likes the music. We have hopes for him to become a musician and to carry the tradition on."

The Original Oompah Band

German Dance Music, Tivydale

By Labor Day the ground cover in the rolling Hill Country of Central Texas has turned a golden brown. Even the live oaks, juniper, and cedar trees have a tawny hue. The farmers tending their wheat, oat, and hay fields hope for rain after a more than a month of blistering heat and drought. When I arrive at the Texas Hills Sporting Range nestled in the small community of Tivydale about fifte

Texas Hills Sporting Range, site of the 51st Reunion of the Gillespie County Old Teamsters Association, Tivydale, Texas, September 1, 1986

Original Oompah Band (left to right: Larry Ottmers, Jim Hartmann, Chrissy Stuewe, and Dianne Pehl McManigle) at the 51st Reunion of the Gillespie County Old Teamsters Association, Tivydale, Texas, September 1, 1986

miles west of Fredericksburg, the fifty-first annual reunion of the Gillespie County Old Teamster's Association is already underway. The six-piece Original Oompah Band is playing "Westphalia Waltz." About a half dozen couples are on the dance floor, a concrete slab under a long corrugated metal awning. Some sit and talk with their families and friends around picnic tables; others cluster together for dominoes. About 80 percent of the people there are speaking a distinct Texas dialect of German, reminiscing about their ancestors, who hauled freight to and from San Antonio with ox-drawn wagons or teams of horses and mules.

Ninety-eight-year-old Hugo Usner, the oldest in attendance, says the spirit of the reunion is "*Gemütlichkeit* . . . a feeling that doesn't translate well into English. It's letting life go as it is and not being concerned about anything . . . let's live for the moment a little bit." Like his forbears who worked as teamsters during the period from the settling of Fredericksburg in 1846 to the coming of the railroad in 1913, Usner hauled cotton and grain but also lumber and dry goods. The first Old Teamsters Reunion was held July 21, 1905, and Usner is one of the few surviving freight drivers.

About Usner, an eighty-one-year-old woman, who introduces herself as Mrs. Felix Heep, recalls, "A couple of years ago at the reunion here, they were trying to see who all was here that had ever driven horses, teamed the horses. So they said, 'Everybody who has driven at least one horse, stand up.' Well . . . three-fourths of the people stood up. 'Two horses,' well, most stayed standing. When it got down to three horses, many had to sit down. They kept on going, and Hugo Usner just kept standing. They got up to twelve horses, and Hugo was still standing by himself, and they said, 'Hugo, how many did you drive?' and he said, 'I drove eighteen horses at one time.' Someone called out, 'Well, Hugo, you know you're getting up in years. Are you sure you're remembering it correctly?' And Hugo answered, 'Yeah, it was eighteen horses.' And the other man asked, 'You sure it wasn't nine one way and nine back home?' And Hugo insisted it was eighteen, so that's the story."

Heep's father came from Germany to Texas in the late 1800s and worked as a teamster, and her husband, while he wasn't a freight driver per se, was a blacksmith who repaired their wagons. "I like everything about the reunion," she says, "the open-pit barbecue, the German potato salad, the beans, the beer, the pies, all the table dressing and home-baked breads. Dancing starts at 2 p.m. There's a short business meeting at three, but that never lasts past three-thirty

51st Reunion of the Gillespie County Old Teamsters Association, Tivydale, Texas, September 1, 1986

Albert Meier performing with the Original Oompah Band at the 51st Reunion of the Gillespie County Old Teamsters Association, Tivydale, Texas, September 1, 1986

51st Reunion of the Gillespie County
Old Teamsters Association, Tivydale,
Texas, September 1, 1986

when the dancing starts up again. Couples like to dance the schottische, the Paul Jones, and the Herr Schmidt. The evening meal is from six to seven, and then, more dancing for about another hour. Everybody is having a good old-time get together . . . a lot of visiting, a lot of storytelling, a lot of enjoying."

THE HEYDAY OF THE ORIGINAL OOMPAH BAND was from the mid-1930s to about 1960, when its founders died and the members of the group went their separate ways. In the early 1980s, James Hartmann, director of the Fredericksburg Chamber of Commerce, revived the name of the group and invited local musicians to join him, some of whom had performed in other bands, most notably the legendary Pehl's Oom-pah Band. All were steeped in the traditional German music they heard grow-ing up.

"I started playing music in the fifth grade when I was ten years old," Dianne Pehl McManigle (born 1960) recalls. "I was handed my grandfather's

Dancers at the 51st Reunion of the
Gillespie County Old Teamsters
Association, Tivydale, Texas, September
1, 1986

trumpet and was expected to learn to play the instrument at school. When I
was getting ready to go to high school, I switched to alto saxophone. It was the
summer after I finished the eighth grade. I was in the band all through high
school, and after I graduated, Mr. Hartmann asked me to play in the Original
Oompah Band that he was putting together."

Hartmann was from a musical family. "My grandfather had a German band
in the late 1800s, early 1900s, so it's been a tradition—that and singing—that's
been going on for quite some time. Like everything else, it's been kind of slowly
dying out. This was the last real German band that we had left, and we only
have two German choirs left. At one time we had seventeen German choirs in
Fredericksburg. Some of the choirs are mixed and consist of more than fifty
people of all ages and walks of life. Others are *Männerchöre*—men's choirs that
traditionally have performed at *Sängerfeste*—singing festivals."

Hartmann was a consummate musician. He played the trumpet, bought
the sheet music, organized arrangements, and got the bookings for the band.
He wanted to carry on the legacy of his mentor, Felix Pehl. "I played with Mr.
Pehl back when I was in high school. Pehl played the trumpet and cornet, and

Old Teamsters Reunion parade, Fredericksburg, Texas, ca. 1949–53, Courtesy Gillespie County Historical Society

Old Teamsters Reunion parade, Fredericksburg, Texas, ca. 1949–53, Courtesy Gillespie County Historical Society

his brother Alfred played the bass drum. I guess I started with Pehl's Old Time Band in 1954 and played through 1957 with him. Then I dropped out when I went to college because I couldn't make the performances anymore. I came back in 1978, I think, and started in again, playing with him. They were kind of down and disorganized at the time, and a lot of the music they were playing was being played by ear. So I went in and wrote the music and got some people

Old Teamsters Reunion band (left to right: performer unknown, _____ Ahrens, Chester Klearner, Hugo Klearner), ca. September 7, 1953, Courtesy Gillespie County Historical Society

who couldn't play it by ear, but they could read music." Many of the songs the Original Oompah Band performed came from the *Little German Band Book,* arranged and compiled by K. Echtner, and included polkas such as "Ach Ich Bin so Müde," "Lott is Tot," "Du Bist Verrückt, Mein Kind," and "Katarina," as well as "Die Melodie" schottische and "Hamburger Waltz."

Hartmann assembled the best musicians he could find. In addition to Dianne Pehl McManigle, he enlisted Larry Ottmers on baritone (euphonium), Albert Meier on bass (sousaphone), Chrissy Stuewe on alto saxophone, and Anthony Hartman on drums. The Original Oompah Band performed at the annual Old Teamsters Reunion, as well as at the Turn Verein, a social hall in Fredericksburg; anniversaries; birthday parties; and the racetrack on the Gillespie County Fairgrounds.

"At the horse races, they had a bandstand in the middle of the bleachers overlooking the finish line. And we'd play in between races," McManigle remembers. "Just like they did decades before us."

Larry Ottmers praises Hartmann for recognizing the potential of having a local German band in Fredericksburg but speculates that he was "probably

Little German Band Book, songbook used by the Original Oompah Band, arranged and compiled by K. Echtner

Sheet music for "Ach Ich Bin So Müde," polka performed by the Original Oompah Band, from the *Little German Band Book*, arranged and compiled by K. Echtner

twenty years too early. While few tourists came to Fredericksburg in the 1980s, it's really booming now. But unfortunately, there are no German bands today."

When asked why the interest in traditional music has declined, McManigle replies, "The leadership isn't there. The kids are still playing the instruments in school, in the marching band. What they need is someone to step forward and help them realize what their cultural heritage really means. But fewer people speak German, and without the language, the music has less appeal."

At the Old Teamsters Reunion, Hartmann points out, "You'd see people standing around, everybody walking from table to table visiting . . . while we were playing you'd see couples getting up, you see a man going across the hall to dance with another woman, the ladies getting up and going to see a man they want to dance with, they go dance with him, and you'd see the kids following along. And today there aren't as many kids going to events like this."

The Old Teamsters Reunion still convenes annually on Labor Day, but it has moved indoors to the Disabled American Veterans (DAV) Hall on US Highway 87 North, two miles outside Fredericksburg. Charles Feller, whose two uncles were freight drivers and who has been president of the Old Teamsters Association for about ten years, says, "We like the air conditioning. It's hot at the beginning of September. But the celebration hasn't changed much. Most of us are up in years, but we've got one who's twenty-five years old and this year we're adding a couple more young people. There's still a lot of dancing. The band is different. These days, we usually have the Hill Country Boys, a group of local musicians from around here, and they play some German oompah (brass band) music, but mostly it's country music—two-steps, polkas, and waltzes."

For German oompah music to continue, like other traditions, there must be a base of family and community support, a mechanism for passing cultural knowledge from one generation to the next. Certainly the Old Teamsters Reunion offers that opportunity, but among younger generations, the stories about the past and perhaps other related traditions such as foodways may ultimately endure more than the music. "To keep it going," Dianne Pehl McManigle says, "there needs be some of the old timers around who can interest the young people coming up."

John Henry "Bones" Nobles

Bones Percussion, Beaumont

In the living room of his white clapboard house in Beaumont, John Henry Nobles is light on his feet, moving from foot to foot in a shuffle or tap step. He is pleased to meet me after talking to me three times on the telephone earlier in the evening. I'd never been to Beaumont before, and finding his house in the dark is difficult. I explain to him that I had gotten his contact information from a librarian at the Institute of Texan Cultures, which produces the annual Texas Folklife Festival in San Antonio, where he has performed on different occasions.

Beaumont, Texas, November 12, 2010

Driving to, Beaumont, Texas,
November 12, 2011

Nobles reaches into a drawer in his china cabinet and takes out a pair of "bones," a handcrafted musical instrument he's made from the ribs of a cow. To play them, he places them on both sides of his middle finger, the seven-inch convex surfaces facing each other, so that about two-thirds of their length lies along his palm while the remainder extends above his fingers on the backside of his hand. His wrist is loose. When he shakes his hand back and forth, the bones click in a rapid rhythm and percussive sound. As he demonstrates, he talks about his life. He points to a portrait of his wife Virgie and his daughters Gloria and Ethel, whose lives are chronicled through snapshots framed on the walls and neatly arranged on tables and shelves alongside his trinkets, knickknacks, ceramic plates, and souvenirs of his travels and performances in schools, nightclubs, and festivals. The "click-it-y" sound of his bones punctuates his stories with improvised rhythms that go late into the night.

JOHN HENRY NOBLES JR. was born in Opp, Alabama on April 18, 1902. His father, John Henry Nobles, was a preacher, and his mother, Pateroney Lee, was part Cherokee and Choctaw Indian. As a boy, he helped out on the sharecropper farm his parents worked and was also able to make a little extra money by shining shoes in town. "It was a nickel for a shine," he said, "but it was always two boys, one working against the other, one shining one shoe, the other shining the other shoe, and the one who shined the best got the nickel. If you couldn't pop the rag and give a *hoodledoodlee,* you didn't get anything. Well, I made sure I was the one going to get that nickel and I could pop that rag so loud I sounded like a buck dancer."

Nobles made his first set of bones when he was nine years old. "I don't care how much rhythm we had," he said, "we didn't have any way to let it out. My dad was making fifty cents a day. Three dollars for six days. There wasn't any money to buy musical instruments. The only way for us to let out our rhythm out was to find us some bones, but the fact is we didn't use bones at first. We cut our rulers at school at the six-inch mark and made us two little sticks to knock and that would give us our vent.

"Bones" Nobles's house, Beaumont, Texas, November 12, 2011

"Bones" Nobles in his living room,
Beaumont, Texas, 1985

"Well, after a while, some of them boys got a little combo going and I wanted to play with them. One boy had a Jew's harp, a rub board, and I was the bones player.

"See, I found this old cow, and the buzzard done cleaned him up and the weather had done cleaned him up, too, and had made them bones white. I went and got me a saw and sawed me off some bones. That put me above them boys who only had sticks. They kept asking me, 'Johnny, where'd you get them bones?' And I'd say, 'A man done come through here from up the country and gave them to me.'

"I went out there and cut me a bunch of bushes and covered up that old cow so that they couldn't find it, and I was kind of unique. So they had to use me in the band."

To prepare his bones, Nobles cooked them with a "secret process" and then rubbed them with a special salve. "I process these bones," he said. "I put a salve in them. It takes about two months to get a set of bones where they'll give you the right sound. I can play myself or with a band. You have to follow that beat."

Nobles could play any kind of rhythm, from African and Latin to Caribbean, bluegrass, and country and western. He loved Zydeco, a music that originated among the Creoles of southwestern Louisiana, melding the influences of Cajun accordion tunes and African American blues with Afro-Caribbean rhythms. Zydeco is a highly rhythmic music with a fast tempo that is usually dominated by a button or piano accordion accompanied by *frottoir* or scrub-board played by stroking spoons or bottle openers on its pressed, corrugated steel surface to create a percussive sound that is similar to the clacking of bones.

Brought to Texas by Creoles looking for better jobs, Zydeco took hold in the cities of Houston and Beaumont, where L. C. Donatto, Lonnie Mitchell, and

"Bones" Nobles's daughter, Gloria Beasley, Beaumont, Texas, November 12, 2010

Gloria Beasley playing her father's bones, Beaumont, Texas, November 12, 2011

"Bones" Nobles, Beaumont, Texas, circa mid-1980s, Courtesy Gloria Beasley

In Loving Memory
of
Mr. John Henry Nobles

April 18, 1902   **"Bones"**   *October 9, 1997*

Saturday, October 18, 1997
1:00 P.M.

Sunlight Baptist Church
1287 Cedar Street - Beaumont, Texas

The Reverend G. W. Daniels
Pastor

Funeral brochure for John Henry
"Bones" Nobles, October 18, 1997

the legendary Clifton Chenier performed often at house parties, church parish halls, and nightclubs. Some musicians relocated to Texas, and others, when they came to the state, hired sidemen like "Bones" Nobles to accompany them.

Nobles moved to Beaumont in 1922, the year he married his wife, Virgie. For most of his adult life, Nobles worked as a truck driver and later owned a BBQ restaurant. Over the years he played occasional shows with another Beaumont musician, bluesman and singer/guitar player Richard Earl, and was often invited to participate in festivals. One of his favorite stories that he liked to tell was about the time a "white girl from Lamar College" stopped him and started asking questions. "She called out, 'Lookee here, Mister Bones,' and I said, 'What you see?' 'Why is one of your bones white and that one black?' And I asked her, 'Why are you white and I'm black?' She said, 'Just go on with the show,' and I explained, 'I didn't make them. Them bones are white when I got them. These bones are black when I got them. So, the good master put color where he want it. I got nothing to do with that. White and black have a different pitch; the black ones, sharper, keener. I play them together. The black and white get along mighty fine when I put them together. You hear that rhythm?'"

Nobles felt he was a teacher and that his music and stories could help people understand each other better. He especially enjoyed playing for children and made frequent appearances at local schools. John Henry "Bones" Nobles died October 9, 1997, at age ninety-five.

Today, his daughter Gloria Beasley still likes to play her father's bones for friends and family at home. While there are no more bones players in Beaumont, she is pleased that the interest in her father and his instrument has spread nationwide. He was featured in the *Newsletter of the Rhythm Bones Society* in 2008 and has been recognized at Bones Fest in St. Louis, where bones players from around the country gather for workshops, historical exhibits, and public performances.

Yani Rose Keo

Cambodian Music and Dance, Houston

Hundreds of people crowd into the Cambodian New Year's celebration at J. B.'s Entertainment Center at 3730 Scott Street in Houston's Third Ward. Nationally known for the blues and jazz artists who have performed there, J. B.'s is an unlikely place for the Cambodian community to gather, but as Yani Rose Keo, vice chairperson of the program committee, explains, "The reason we at J. B.'s, the temple wouldn't hold that many Cambodians. More than seven thousand Cambodians in Houston. We need a big hall, you know, and that's why we rent that hall. I know the father of the owner of J. B.'s and he charges us 50 percent less than other groups because we are a refugee group. That hall can hold seven hundred, but not only from Houston tonight—we have Dallas, Austin, even Louisiana." Inside J. B.'s, long rows of tables point toward the stage. Every seat is occupied. Latecomers stand in the back of the sprawling room, leaning against the walls or milling among the tables. Some sit in the aisles on the floor.

1985 is the Year of the Ox, and after welcoming remarks by the president of the Cambodian Association, the eight-piece Neak Poon Musical Group begins to play. Dancers in traditional costumes take the stage for the Adoration Dance, followed by the Parasol Dance, Parrot Dance, Ken Dance, and "Escape to Freedom," a dramatic recreation of the brutal onslaught of the Khmer Rouge. "Escape to Freedom" unfolds in a burst of action. Fog machines puff out a hazy glow as a group of refugees weaves in and out of what appears to be jungle bushes and vines. The sounds of drums echo through the room; a lone male makes his way to the center of the stage and falls to his knees, agitated and distraught, breaking down into a blood-curdling scream that silences the audience. Tears run down his cheeks. Everyone in the room feels his pain.

Driving to Houston, November 12, 2010

Bus Stop in front of the Alliance for Multicultural Services, 6440 Hillcroft Avenue, Houston, Texas, where Yani Rose Keo works. November 12, 2010

YANI ROSE KEO came to Houston on October 13, 1975, to reunite with her husband, whom she thought had been killed by the Khmer Rouge. "We left Cambodia together with our youngest son on a private plane to Bangkok two weeks before Pol Pot took over," she recalls, "but once we got there my husband said he must go back. He said he did not do anything wrong. He cannot leave his job. He was the director of the railroad. And I said, 'Okay, you can go back.' And I left with my son for Paris, where my three other children were already in school. That was in April, and then I heard nothing from my husband for more than five months. But I knew what happened in Cambodia. Many, many people were killed. I thought my husband was dead. I was so angry. I don't have money. I hate the world. Finally, in Paris, I got a job as a pediatric nurse, and one day, my boss told me I have a phone call. I don't want any phone calls. It was so hard for me. My boss said, 'Please sit down and listen to this call.' I heard this Cambodian voice. He said his name and he told me the date of our marriage and the children's ages and names. And it clicked in my mind, 'Who know my root?' The last thing he said was he missed the plane when he was supposed to go back. They took him to

Yani Rose Keo at her desk at the
Alliance for Multicultural Services,
Houston, Texas, November 12, 2010

Yani Rose Keo in her office at the
Alliance for Multicultural Services,
Houston, Texas, November 12, 2010

Yani Rose Keo's office at the Alliance for Multicultural Services, Houston, Texas, November 12, 2010

a refugee camp in Bangkok, and he stuck in the camp like a slave, not enough food to eat until the Catholic charities sponsor him out. That's when he come to Houston."

The day after Keo arrived in Houston, she started working as a volunteer to help Cambodian refugees, first with the United Way, the Red Cross, and Catholic Charities and then in the Houston Independent School District. Born near the Royal Palace in Phnom Penh, Cambodia, October 4, 1939, she was a well-educated paraprofessional fluent in English, Khmer, French, Thai, Lao, and Vietnamese. Her mother was a Khmer classical dancer who performed in the Royal Ballet in the court of the king and queen of Cambodia. Using stylized movements and gestures to tell stories, much like pantomime, classical dancers never speak or sing; they dance with a slight smile but never open their mouths. Each hand gesture represents different natural elements, such as fruit, flowers, and leaves, to convey different thoughts and concepts. Classical Khmer dance is choreographed to the music played by a *pinpeat* orchestra, consisting of predominantly percussion instruments, including the *Roneat Ek* (a high bamboo xylophone with twenty-one keys mounted on a curved box resonator), *Roneat Thung* (a low bamboo xylophone with sixteen keys), *Kong Vong Touch* and *Kong Vong Thom* (two sets, one large, one small, a total of thirty-three tuned gongs suspended horizontally from rattan frames), *Sampho* (a two-sided drum), *Skor Thom* (two large drums played with heavy wooden mallets), and *Sralai* (a double-reed wind instrument). While Cambodian musicians and dancers are called "classical" because of their formal training, they nonetheless carry on time-honored traditions, many of which are not written down but are transmitted orally from generation to generation.

During the Pol Pot regime, between 1975 and 1979, more than 90 percent of all Khmer classical dancers and musicians perished. Doctors, teachers, intellectuals, and performers of Khmer arts were imprisoned, tortured, and killed. "Once I leave Cambodia I have no contact with any of my family," Keo laments. "It was not until 1991 that I could go back. I look for my family in refugee camps in Thailand and I almost got killed myself. The Thai soldiers found me in the camp. They kick me around. I'm lucky to be alive to get out. I was looking for my mother. I go to Cambodia and find out everyone in my family and my husband's family dead. We don't know how they died, where they died, what we heard was those people killed my family with an axe. It's terrible. The pain in my heart never heals. I pray for my family. I pray for the innocent

Wat Buddharangsey Cambodian Buddhist Temple, 15211 Sellers Road, Houston, Texas, November 13, 2010

Yani Rose Keo (third from left) praying at the Wat Buddharangsey Cambodian Buddhist Temple, Houston, Texas, November 13, 2010

Yani Rose Keo praying at the Wat Buddharangsey Cambodian Buddhist Temple, Houston, Texas, November 13, 2010

Yani Rose and Saoroth Keo on their
wedding day, Phnom Penh, Cambodia,
July 31, 1953, Courtesy Yani Rose Keo

Yani Rose Keo's daughter Nanda Pok, son Sorith Keo, and friend Saing Lort, performing at Yani Rose Keo's fiftieth wedding anniversary party, July 31, 2003, Courtesy Yani Rose Keo

Cambodians. That's why for thirty-five years I've been helping people."

Keo founded the Cambodian Association of Houston in 1976 to provide social services and job training for refugees, and she was one of the cofounders of the Wat-Buddharangsey Cambodian temple. Then, in 1979, she started a Cambodian dance company. "At first, I just have my four children dance, and it slowly grow. At the time we don't have any traditional clothes. I make them myself by hand to preserve the culture. After that, my children grow up and we organized a band. My son-in-law, Daly Moul, played lead guitar and was the leader of the band; my son, Soudeth Keo on drums, Sam Phup Kou on keyboard, and my other son, Sorith Keo, on bass."

"We played traditional Cambodian music," Sorith says, "plus Western music. Most of the songs when we start playing are about how we got out of the Communism regime, the Khmer Rouge, and after that the songs are about how we dealt with it and how we have to go on, go forward. Most of the time, my brother-in-law wrote lyrics. I put the music together. We can forgive, but not forget."

In addition to traditional and contemporary music, Sorith was also a member of the group of classical Cambodian musicians that his mother organized.

Cambodian New Year's Celebration,
J. B.'s Entertainment Center, Houston,
Texas, April 13, 1985

Cambodian New Year's Celebration, J. B.'s Entertainment Center, Houston, Texas, April 13, 1985

"I played the *Chapei Veng,* a two-string guitar," Sorith says. "The *Chapei Veng* is sometimes made from a coconut wrapped with snakeskin. I first started learning music when I was eight or nine back home from my uncle's friends who were musicians. In Cambodia, the musical ensemble usually has the *Chapai Veng,* the *Pai-ar* [double-reed bamboo flute], *Slek* [single-leaf instrument], *Tro Khmer* [three-string fiddle], *Khse Diev* [single-string lute], *Chihhing* [pair of antique cymbals], and *Skor Arak* [small drum]. But in Houston, it was difficult to find people who could play all the instruments that were part of a traditional Khmer musical ensemble."

The live music performed at weddings and at the annual Cambodian New Year's celebration held annually on April 13, Sorith says, is based on traditional sounds but often played with Western instruments. "By necessity, the tradition must take a new form, but we do our best to remember. The New Year's celebration begins in the morning at our Buddhist temple. We practice Mahanikay Buddhism that involves chanting and prayer, followed by a food offering—curry, fish, stew, and a lot different dishes the Cambodians prepare. They offer it to the monk, and after the monk finishes his lunch, everybody starts eating. Then at 6 p.m. the celebration continues with music and dance."

"After the structured program," Sorith explains, "then our live band starts, and just about everyone in the hall got up to dance [contemporary Western-style dancing]." Yani Keo says that the classical musicians and the contemporary band rarely perform today because there are fewer young people interested, although the scope of her work has expanded. "We changed our name to the Alliance for Multicultural Community Services. We help so many refugees all over the world."

Leaving Houston, November 13, 2010

Although it is more difficult to engage the younger generation, Keo is nonetheless committed to the preservation of Cambodian cultural traditions. "We still sponsor musicians and dancers, but there are not enough teachers here. We don't have all of the traditional instruments, but we recognize the importance of the music. You need your own music and your own culture, even if we can only hear it in recordings. You have to know your root, where you come from. You should not forget where you from. It doesn't matter. You got the citizenship paper. Your body, your blood, it's still who you are. It's very important, I taught all the refugees here. I said, 'Welcome to the United States. Take something good from this country—your freedom, but you have to respect the law. One thing you should not forget—who you are, who's your root.' That's what I tell everybody because this is me."

Appendix

Traditional Music in Texas *Radio Series**

1984

Seminole-Kiowa Indian Hilton Queton leads a gourd dance in Irving.

Kiowa Indian Joe Big Bow from Anadarko, Oklahoma plays ceremonial songs on his handcrafted wooden flute in Dallas.

Alexander H. Moore, at age eighty-five, performs his distinctive piano style that combines ragtime, boogie-woogie, and barrelhouse blues in Oak Cliff.

Ennis accordionist Jodie Mikula and his three sons highlight a Czech polka dance at the Sokol Hall in Dallas.

Rocky Elliot and the Blue Ridge Bluegrass Jamboree perform at a community center in Wylie.

The Light Crust Doughboys bring their Western swing to Southfork Ranch in Plano.

Eli Davidsohn plays his accordion and sings Yiddish songs for his wife and daughter in Richardson.

Beto Vasquez and his Conjunto play at a Mexican American dance at Rob's Place in East Dallas.

Trio Los Olmos sings at a family reunion and barbecue in a Fort Worth backyard.

Dave Romo and his Mariachi Social perform at a benefit for a needy family at a Knights of Columbus Hall in Dallas.

In his living room in Dallas, harmonica player A. W. Breeland plays the songs he learned as a child in Mississippi.

Fiddler Jim "Texas Shorty" Chancellor jams with Dallas area musicians and demonstrates the Texas style of fiddling.

1986

More than two hundred men, women, and children gather together at the Bethel Primitive Baptist Church in McMahan for the 85th Southwest Texas Sacred Harp Singing Convention.

Lonnie Mitchell plays zydeco in the kitchen of his home in Houston.

Czech accordionist Julius Vita sings for family and friends in Wicker Feed store in Seymour, celebrating the 88th Old Settlers' Reunion.

Allen Thibodeaux and the French Ramblers play Cajun music at a dance in Groves.

Robert Shaw, the last surviving member of the legendary Santa Fe group of barrelhouse pianists, plays hot roadhouse music in his home in Austin.

Fiddler Troy Everidge plays jigs, reels, and waltzes at a house party in Granbury.

The New Ulm Oompah Band features German accordionist Davey Gross and his wife Norma, with their longtime friends Helen and Leo Michlitz.

Juanita and Maria Mendoza sing love songs in the *ranchera* style at their home in San Antonio.

The Woloski family sing traditional Yiddish songs and talk about Spanish-speaking Jews in McAllen.

Narciso Martinez plays *norteño* accordion in San Benito.

Osceola Mays in Dallas recites poems and sings spirituals that she learned from her mother, Azalean Douglas, and her grandmother, Laura Walker, who was ten years old when the Emancipation Proclamation was signed to end slavery.

*Researched and produced by Alan Govenar with support from Documentary Arts, Inc. and the National Endowment for the Arts for broadcast on KERA, 90.1 FM and the Longhorn Radio Network. Narration and editing by Nancy Lamb.

Howard Dee "Wes" Westmoreland III and three generations of his family play breakdown fiddling at the Gustine Homecoming, Reunion, and Fiddling Contest.

Yani Rose Keo and members of her community celebrate the Cambodian New Year in Houston.

1988

Lavada Durst, better known as "Dr. Hepcat," performs his piano blues in Austin.

L. C. Donatto and the Silver Slippers Zydeco band in Houston perform Creole music with fast-syncopated rhythms.

In Beaumont, John Henry "Bones" Nobles plays his hand-made set of bones, cut from the ribs of cows and specially treated.

Guitar maker W. W. "Skinny" Trammell talks about his craft and jams with friends in his living room in Lone Star.

Fiddler and fiddle maker Math Deatherage performs with his wife and daughter in Abilene.

Bajo sexto maker Alberto Macias works in his shop in San Antonio and sings children's songs to his wife and daughter.

Accordionist Valerio Longoria demonstrates his distinctive style of *conjunto* music in San Antonio.

Corridista Carlos Olivas Jimenez plays accordion and sings in Redford on the Rio Grande.

Lydia Mendoza plays her twelve-string guitar and sings *corridos* and *rancheras* in Houston.

The Original Oompah Band performs at the 51st Old Teamsters Reunion in Tivydale outside Fredericksburg.

Miguel Pedraza plays a three-hundred-year-old Piro drum and sings Tigua Indian chants at Ysleta del sur Pueblo in El Paso.

John Burrus from Stephenville sings cowboy songs and country hymns, accompanying himself on guitar and harmonica.

Bill Neely from Austin plays the country blues learned while picking cotton as a boy near McKinney.

Acknowledgments

The people I met while writing this book are as varied as the places I traveled. I will always be grateful to them and their families for sharing their music and opening their lives to me.

The support of Documentary Arts and the National Endowment for the Arts afforded me the opportunity to revisit where my work began more than twenty-five years ago and to deepen my study of the performers and the musical traditions they carry on.

My ongoing dialogue with Betty Carter challenged me through numerous revisions, and her recommendations for further reading pointed me in new directions. Kip Lornell offered suggestions that strengthened my discussion of the ways musical styles evolve over time.

Paddy Bowman broadencd my understanding of how folk traditions interface with the learning process through the education guide she developed, which accompanies this book and is available on the website (www.everydaymusiconline.org) designed by Daniel Dunnam and Kelli Anderson. Alan Hatchett, Blas Garcia and Jason Spinos edited audio and video segments. Katy Parker of Coupralux scanned and color-corrected photographs.

Over the years my family has provided the strongest support of my efforts. My wife, Kaleta Doolin, my son Alex, and my daughter Breea, who joined me on different occasions, separately and together, always enhanced my journey around Texas, helping to keep my mind sharp and my spirit fresh.

For Further Reading, Listening & Viewing

Introduction

Hartman, Gary. *The History of Texas Music*. College Station, TX: Texas A&M University Press, 2008. Hartman provides a thorough overview of the history of Texas music, investigating the roots of different musical traditions by highlighting the careers of some of the state's most influential performers.

Lornell, Kip. *Exploring American Folk Music*. Jackson, MS: University Press of Mississippi, 2012. Lornell chronicles the vast scope of folk music in the United States with detailed information on different traditional styles.

Nye, Naomi Shiab, ed. *Is This Forever, or What? Poems and Paintings from Texas*. New York: Greenwillow, 2004. In a spunky introduction, Nye informs readers that she compiled this volume to highlight "the beautiful diversity, the multiplicity of our state."

Turner, Robin Montana. *Texas Traditions*. New York: Little Brown, 1996. Although currently out of print, it covers, in a number of chapters illustrated with original art, archival photographs, and sidebar material, various threads of Texas culture, including rodeos, music, and dance.

Julius Vita

Hyde, Heidi Smith. *Mendel's Accordion*. Minneapolis: Kar-Ben, 2007. When Mendel realizes he must emigrate from Eastern Europe, he takes his beloved klezmer (accordion) with him. Mendel's great-grandson, Samuel, finds the klezmer, fixes it, and forms a band of his own. Based on a true story.

Nislick, June Levitt. *Zayda Was a Cowboy*. Philadelphia: Jewish Publication Society, 2005. Zayda (the Yiddish word for grandfather) tells his grandchildren about his rich, and often humorous, life after entering the United States and Texas through the Port of Galveston at the beginning of the twentieth century. Although Zayda came from Russia (not Czechoslovakia, like Julius Vita's family), his story provides a window to the immigrant experience through the Port of Galveston.

Sís, Peter. *The Wall: Growing Up behind the Iron Curtain*. New York: Frances Foster Books/Farrar, 2007. Author and illustrator Sís shares, through drawings and diaries, his life in his native Czechoslovakia from childhood to young adulthood and eventual immigration to the United States in 1984.

Stoffels, Karlijin. *Heartsinger*. New York: Arthur L. Levine Books, 2009. This Norwegian import, a book that is rooted in both fantasy and realism, sings a love story through music, bringing together Mee, a singer, and Mitou, an accordion player.

Texas-Czech, Bohemian-Moravian Bands (CD, Arhoolie 7026) contains recordings made between 1929 and the late 1950s that help to establish the historical context of the music performed by Julius Vita. Readers may also be interested in hearing the *Traditional Music in Texas* radio segments on Jodie Mikula and his three sons performing at a Czech dance at the Sokol Hall in Dallas. Sokol is an international organization, founded in 1862 in the Czech lands that later became Czechoslovakia (now Czech Republic and Slovak Republic). In the United States, member chapters of the Sokol organization not only host Czech dances but also offer physical training in gymnastics and other athletics and promote cultural awareness and family-oriented activities.

John Burrus

Hopkinson, Deborah. *Home on the Range: John A. Lomax and His Cowboy Songs*. Illus. S. D. Schindler. New York: Putnam, 2009. Although the title, ironically, indicates that "Home on the Range" is a cowboy song (it isn't and the author makes that point clear), the text follows John Lomax and his attempts to record and popularize the cowboy songs of the west.

Krull, Kathleen, ed. *I Hear America Singing: Folk Songs for American Families.* Illus. Allen Garns. New York: Knopf, 2009. This comprehensive volume, originally titled *Gonna Sing My Head Off: Folk Songs for Children,* includes some cowboy songs. *Songs of the Wild West* (with text by Alan Alexrod and arranged by Dan Fox, published in 1991 by Simon and Schuster), an out-of-print edition, offers additional cowboy songs (some by cowboys and some about cowboys) with arrangements suitable for beginner and intermediate musicians.

Sabbeth, Alex. *Rubber-Band Banjos and a Java Jive Bass: Projects and Activities on the Science of Music and Sound.* Illus. Laurel Aiello. New York: Wiley, 1997. Combining science, music, and crafts, Sabbeth provides instructions for making a variety of instruments, including a harmonica and a number of string instruments.

Saunders, Tom B IV. *The Texas Cowboys: Cowboy of the Lone Star State—A Photographic Portrayal.* Photographs by David R. Stoecklein. Ketchum, ID: Stoecklein Publishing, 1997. This large, coffee-table book offers a history of cowboys in Texas but concentrates on the work they do today across the state through twenty-three operating ranches. Most pertinent to John Burrus's story is an out-of-print book, *Cowboy Life on the Texas Plains* by Margaret Rector and published by Texas A&M University Press in 1982. All photographs here are by cowboy photographer Bob Rector, including the first Cowboy Reunion in Stamford in the early 1930s, a project Rector directed.

Recordings of John Burrus with detailed notes are available on the CD *Cowboy Songs & Country Hymns* (Documentary Arts 1010). The CDs *Cowboy Songs on Folkways* (Smithsonian Folkways SFW40043); Buck Ramsey, *Hittin' the Trail* (Smithsonian Folkways SFW50002); and Tex-i-an Boys, *Songs of Texas* (Smithsonian Folkways SFW5328) elaborate the historical and national context of Burrus' music.

Osceola Mays

Giovanni, Nikki. *On My Journey Now: Looking at African-American History Through the Spirituals.* Boston: Candlewick, 2007. Using her strong poetic voice, Giovanni discusses the role of music in the lives of African Americans who decided "I am going to go through it and make it a song." She begins with songs of slavery and continues through music in the Civil War. She discusses the influence of spirituals today and most probably tomorrow. Includes complete lyrics of the songs mentioned.

Govenar, Alan. *Osceola: Memories of a Sharecropper's Daughter.* Illus. Shane W. Evans. New York: Hyperion, 2000. Through oral interviews with Osceola Mays, Govenar gives readers a full version of her life, beginning with her hardscrabble childhood and continuing through her life in Dallas. Presently out of print.

Hoberman, Mary Ann. *Miss Mary Mack: A Hand-Clapping Rhyme.* Boston: Little Brown, 1998. Here's a pictorial version of the rhyme Osceola Mays was sharing with children at the beginning of the chapter. Includes directions for participating in hand clapping and singing the simple tune.

Meyer, Carolyn. *White Lilacs.* San Diego: Harcourt, 1993. Basing her account on a true incident from Quakertown (part of Denton, Texas), Meyer tells of the forced evacuation of Freedomtown of African-Americans so the city could build a park. The setting is the 1930s, when Osceola was growing up about two hundred miles southwest of that town, and shows the attitudes of much of white society towards the African American community during her childhood.

Recordings of Osceola Mays singing spirituals and reciting her poems are available on the CD *Spirituals and Poems* (Documentary Arts 1006). Also, the DVD video *Osceola Mays: Stories, Songs, and Poems* (25 minutes, Documentary Arts, 1996) contains footage of Osceola performing at home, in her church, and at a local Dallas school.

Howard Dee "Wes" Westmoreland III

Landau, Elaine. *Is the Violin for You?* Minneapolis: Lerner, 2011. The difference between the violin and the fiddle is in the playing rather than the instrument. Here, Landau examines what it takes to play the instrument, with particular emphasis on practice.

Sabbeth, Alex. *Rubber-Band Banjos and a Java Jive Bass: Projects and Activities on the Science of Music and Sound.* Illus. Laurel Aiello. New York: Wiley, 1997. Combining science, music, and crafts, Sabbeth provides instructions for making a variety of instruments, including a harmonica and a number of string instruments.

Sullivan, Sarah. *Passing the Music Down.* Illus. Barry Root. Boston: Candlewick, 2010. This small picture book shares the power of music. In West Virginia, a young boy travels to meet Melvin Wine (a renowned fiddler in the area) to learn his art. The boy (Jake

Krak, the youngest musician to win West Virginia's State Fiddling Championship) eventually forms his own band. A concluding author's note provides additional context.

The DVD video *Texas Style* (Directed by Alan Govenar and Pacho Lane, Documentary Arts, 2012) chronicles the growth of the Texas style of fiddling and features the Westmoreland family in interviews, as well as in performances at a fiddle contest in Gustine and at a family reunion. Additional recordings that help to elaborate the historical and cultural context of Texas-style fiddling include Benny Thomasson and Dick Barrett, *Texas Fiddle Legends* (Yazoo 517) and Jim "Texas Shorty" Chancellor (Documentary Arts 1012).

Miguel Pedraza Sr.

Burnett, Carolyn Mitchell. *The First Texans*. Austin: Eakin Press, 1995. Burnett gives a brief overview of seventeen Indian tribes in Texas, devoting one chapter to the Tiguas. Currently out of print.

Ench, Rick and Jay Cravath. *North American Indian Music*. New York: Watts, 2001. Although no mention is made of the Tigua Indians, this general overview of Native American music covers spiritual, social, and secular music. A tangential offering, the first chapter of James Gleick's *The Information* (New York: Pantheon, 2011) provides a detailed interpretation of the historical power of drumming among indigenous peoples.

The Melting Pot: Ethnic Cuisine in Texas. Austin: University of Texas Institute of Texas Cultures, 1997. This out-of-print edition contains easy to follow recipes from various ethnic groups, including one for Tigua Sopa Bread contributed by Miguel Pedraza.

Wright, Bill. *Tiguas: Pueblo Indians of Texas*. El Paso: Texas Western Press, 1993. This monograph includes an essay on the history of the Tigua and presents an evocative series of black and white photographs of landscapes, daily life, and the celebration of the Fiesta de San Antonio.

For current information on the Tiguas, see www.ysletadelsurpueblo.org.

Alexander H. Moore

Myers, Walter Dean. *Blues Journey*. Illus. Christopher Meyers. New York: Holiday House, 2003. Myers opens this collection of original poetry with a detailed explanation of the blues: the rhythm, the subject, and its import for the African American community.

Poems, and the powerful illustrations, cover a variety of topics ranging from racism to general misfortune.

Parker, Robert Andrew. *Piano Starts Here: The Young Art Tatum*. New York: Schwartz & Wade/Random House, 2008. Although Tatum is renowned as a jazz pianist, he, like Alexander Moore, was self-taught. His love for the piano and the sounds he coached from it are both reminiscent of Moore's story.

Igus, Toyomi. *I See the Rhythm*. Illus. Michele Wood. San Francisco: Children's Book Press, 1998. A series of free-verse poems highlight African American music, including blues, rhythm and blues, and ragtime. Each chapter includes a timeline of high points in the musical genre and is accompanied by powerful illustrations filled with color and motion.

W. W. "Skinny" Trammell

Auch, Mary Jane. *Guitar Boy*. New York: Holt, 2010. Thirteen-year-old Travis is pretty much on his own after his mother becomes unable to speak and his father tells Travis to leave. It's only when he meets a gifted guitar craftsman that Travis begins to heal through the twin arts of making music and beautiful instruments.

Blaxland, Wendy. *Guitars*. New York: Marshall Cavendish Benchmark, 2010. As but one entry in the series *How Are They Made?*, this book examines guitars: their history, their construction, and their sales.

VanHecke, Susan. *Raggin,' Jazzin,' Rockin': A History of American Instrument Makers*. Honesdale, PA: Boyds Mill, 2011. Through a cogent text, lavish color photographs, and interesting sidebars, VanHecke traces the history of crafting a number of instruments, with an emphasis on guitars.

Lydia Mendoza

Broyles-González, Yolanda. *My Life in Music (Mi Vida en la Musica); Lydia Mendoza: Norteño Tejano Legacies*. New York: Oxford University Press, 2001.

Mendoza, Lydia, Chris Strachwitz, and James Nicolopolus. *Lydia Mendoza: A Family Autobiography*. Houston: Arte Publico Press, 1993. Both of these biographies provide a thorough overview of Lydia Mendoza's life and career through edited transcriptions of oral accounts and a discussion of song lyrics.

Farrar, Josh. *Rules to Rock By*. New York: Walker, 2010. Annabelle Cabera loves two things: her *abuela* and her band, but when her family moves to Rhode Island, she must leave both. But

Annabelle's determination to start a new group (and her successes and failures) aid in her adjustment to a new home.

McKenzie, Phyllis. *The Mexican Texans.* College Station, TX: Texas A&M University Press, 2004. McKenzie traces the influences of Mexicans living in Texas, beginning with Colonial times and ending with the start of the twenty-first century, including a section on *corridos.*

Recordings of Lydia Mendoza are available on the CDs *The First Queen of Tejano Music* (Arhoolie 392), *La Alondra De La Frontera Con Orqusta Falcon* (Arhoolie 513), *Mal Hombre and Other Original Hits from the 1930s* (Arhoolie 7002), *Vida Mía* (Arhoolie 7008), and *The Best of Lydia Mendoza* (Arhoolie 536). Lydia Mendoza also appears in the documentary DVD video *Chulas Fronteras* (directed by Chris Strachwitz and Les Blank, Brazos Films, 1976).

Original Oompah Band

Watriss, Wendy, Fred Baldwin, and Lawrence Goodwyn. *Coming to Terms: The German Hill Country of Texas.* College Station, TX: Texas A&M University Press, 1991. The black and white photographs in this out-of-print monograph document the rural life and culture among people of German descent in the area around Fredericksburg, Texas.

Lich, Glen E. *The German Texans.* Austin: University of Texas Institute of Texas Cultures, 1996. This out-of-print volume develops the history of German immigration in Texas from the 1830s (when most Germans came from other states) to the influx in 1845 from Europe. It also covers many German folk traditions that were imported by the immigrants. The final chapter discusses the blending of two cultures (German and American) and the gradual disappearance of the German one.

John Henry "Bones" Nobles

Hopkinson, Deborah. *Up Before Daybreak: Cotton and People in America.* New York: Scholastic, 2006. Dealing with all aspects of "king cotton" in the nineteenth and twentieth centuries, Hopkinson includes much information about sharecropping, especially the backbreaking work performed by children.

Strum, James. *Satchel Paige: Striking Out Jim Crow.* New York: Jump at the Sun/Hyperion, 2007. Like John Nobles, Emmet Wilson (who narrates this graphic novel) is the son of a sharecropper. He joins the Negro Baseball League, and the high point of his career is getting a hit off Satchel Paige. But when Wilson is injured, he returns to farming and his struggle against the Jim Crow laws of the South in the mid twentieth century.

The website www.rhythmbones.com explores the history and practice of bones, including practical information on how to make and play the instrument.

Yani Rose Keo

Demi. *Buddha.* New York: Holt, 1996. Demi's hallmark illustrations, dainty ink and watercolor, incorporate gold lines to add to the majesty of this account that begins with Siddhartha's birth and follows his life and teachings. Not only an introduction to the man, *Buddha* incorporates much about the Buddhist religion within its pages.

Ebihara, May B., Carol A. Mortland, and Judy Ledgerwood, eds. *Cambodian Culture Since 1975.* Ithaca, NY: Cornell University Press, 1994. The essays in this book provide an overview of Cambodian immigration to the United States and help to establish the context of Yani Rose Keo's move to the United States.

Keat, Nawuth. *Alive in the Killing Fields: Surviving the Khmer Rouge Genocide.* Washington: National Geographic, 2009. Nawuth Keat's autobiography doesn't shirk from the horrors he endured after the Khmer Rouge invaded his village. Watching the killings and torture, and slaving to the point of starvation, he escapes and, after a harrowing journey through the jungle (eating snakes and monkeys), reaches a refugee camp before immigrating to the United States.

Smith, Icy. *Half Spoon of Rice: A Survival Story of the Cambodian Genocide.* Illus. Sopaul Nhem. Manhattan Beach, CA: East West Discovery Press, 2010. Smith offers a picture book based on survivor stories from those who endured the Khmer Rouge. Young Nat serves as the narrator, and he sees the horrors of death, starvation, and the inescapable cruelty from the Khmer Rouge. He eventually goes to Thailand to a refugee camp; like Yani Keo he immigrates to the United States. A detailed author's note provides much historical background to the period.

Index